Dedicated to the
Munford First A
past, present, and future.

Acknowledgements

Credit for this book belongs to the Lord first, members of River of Life Munford First Assembly of God Church, and especially to those who provided testimonies, photos, and other documents as part of this "labor of love."

This book would not have been possible without the dedication and support of Dorothy (Valentine) Williams, Janice (Valentine) Greathouse, and Peggy (Pinner) Cox. These special servants of God provided most of the background for each chapter and meticulously reviewed each page to help ensure this book represents an accurate portrayal of the church history.

I also appreciate the editorial support provided by John Earl Wells, who reviewed each chapter and offered suggestions in his typical humble and humorous manner.

Special thanks to my wife, Lucinda, who used her God-given skills in transcribing hours of interviews. These transcribed notes were essential in accurately sharing the information provided by members of the church.

River of Life Church
220 Beaver Road
Munford, TN 38058
901-837-8781
www.munfordriveroflife.com

**All profits from the sale of this book are
donated to missions.**

Thank you for reading this historical record of River of Life (First Assembly of God) Church set in our fine city of Munford, Tennessee. As a matter of introduction, let me share with you that I was practically born at the church! My roots run very deep at River of Life and in my hometown of Munford, where I am currently blessed to serve as City Mayor. This church is deeply woven into the fabric of my life. It was here I was challenged to become a student of the Word. It was here I observed honorable men and women live godly lives. It was here I learned that the essence of leadership is servanthood.

The City of Munford was originally called Mt. Zion, named after Mt. Zion Methodist Church which was established in the 1840s. From its inception, church has been the bedrock of our town's purpose and the center of community life. Our town slogan is *Munford is My Kind of Town,* and River of Life Church compliments our town very well. From distributing food to needy families, to participating in local events, to the preaching of the Good News, this church ministers powerfully and effectively to our citizens.

River of Life Church was established on the cusp of the Great Depression in 1929. Those difficult days created a desperation and hunger for the miracle-working power of Jesus. Throughout our history, the people of River of Life have been known for effectual fervent prayer, inspiring music, a heart for world missions, and miraculous healings. As you progress through decades of history, please pause to worship with us along the way. This is more than just the chronicle of a small church in West Tennessee. This is the record of God's great faithfulness to His people, and we say with great confidence, "thus far the Lord has helped us."

I would like to thank my friends Alvin and Lucinda Plexico for their efforts in compiling eighty-five years of personal testimony and historical data to produce this book. I would also like to thank all those who shared their testimonies, photos, and other documents as part of this book. The men and women at this church are more than fellow believers, they're my family in Christ. This book, which represents our shared history, is important in defining the role of River of Life Church in this community for the coming decades or until Jesus comes again.

Dwayne Cole, Mayor
City of Munford, Tennessee

Born from Revival

Raymond Wiseman was in the last stages of tuberculosis when he prayed for God to spare his life so that he could build a church and lead his family members to salvation. In 1928 he brought a tent to Glen Springs in West Tennessee between Drummonds Road and Highway 59 West. During this time, Glen Springs was a resort and recreational area. Reverend Wiseman, assisted by Reverend William Bridges preached every night with only a few in attendance. They survived on bread and blackberries. After three weeks of uneventful meetings, a young man was carried to the tent because he was too sick from illness to stand. After the evangelists prayed, God raised him to his feet.

The healing triggered a tremendous revival that continued for four months. The tent was moved to Crosstown (between Munford and Atoka, Tennessee), where thousands gathered for the services. At the closing of the "Crosstown Revival" a baptismal service was held at Atoka Pond.

Not everyone was pleased with the revival or the church being built as evidenced by a letter dated November 10, 1928, from *Peacemakers for the State of Tennessee* who wrote, "In regards to the church you are getting built it must not go up, because we will protect our state and don't let us have to come out. If so you will regret it." In a separate letter signed by the *Citizens of Munford*, Reverend Wiseman was warned that, "This church must not go up in this place: Instead of it being a peace maker it is a Hell raiser and we don't need it or you in this town…"

Undeterred, 31 charter members set the church in order on February 3, 1929, in the home of Mr. and Mrs. Emery Pinner. Worship services were held in various members' homes until a church building was ready. The congregation raised cotton to help pay for a church building. Women and children pulled cotton stalks to clear the site as the men dug the foundation at the present location at 220 Beaver Road in Munford, TN.

References

Bridges, W. A. (n.d.). *The Amazing Grace of God in the life of Bro. William A. Bridges.*

Munford First Assembly of God (1994). *65th Anniversary Program.*

Rasnake, J. S. (1975). *Stones by the River: A History of the Tennessee District of the Assemblies of God.*

River of Life Assembly of God (2009). *80th Anniversary Program.*

Assembly of God History

The General Council of the Assemblies of God (USA), one of the largest Pentecostal denominations in the United States, was organized in 1914 by a broad coalition of ministers who desired to work together to fulfill common objectives such as sending missionaries and providing fellowship and accountability.

One of the focal points of the emerging Pentecostal movement was known as the Azusa Street revival (1906-09). In the summer of 1906, revival erupted in the newly-formed congregation meeting at the small, run-down Apostolic Faith Mission at 312 Azusa Street in Los Angeles, California. Critics attacked the congregation because its mild-mannered African-American Holiness preacher, William J. Seymour, preached racial reconciliation and the restoration of biblical spiritual gifts. The revival soon became a local sensation, and then attracted thousands of curiosity seekers and pilgrims from around the world.

As the revival rapidly spread, many Pentecostals recognized the need for greater organization and accountability. The founding fathers and mothers of the Assemblies of God met in Hot Springs, Arkansas, on April 2-12, 1914, to promote unity and doctrinal stability, establish legal standing, coordinate the mission enterprise, and establish a ministerial training school. The approximately 300 delegates to the first General Council represented a variety of independent churches and networks of churches, including the "Association of Christian Assemblies" in Indiana and the "Church of God in Christ and in Unity with the Apostolic Faith Movement" from Alabama, Arkansas, Mississippi, and Texas.

From the beginning, evangelism and missions have been central to the identity of the Assemblies of God and have resulted in a continuing growth at home and abroad. In 2007, the Assemblies of God claimed a constituency in the United States of 2,836,174 adherents; 12,311 churches; and 33,622 ministers. The General Council supported 2,691 foreign missionaries and associates working with the broader World Assemblies of God Fellowship, whose adherents numbered more than 57 million.

Source: Brief History of the Assemblies of God. Retrieved from http://ag.org/top/about/History/

Historical events from the 1920s (source: U.S. Census Bureau)

- Presidents of the United States: Calvin Coolidge and Herbert Hoover.
- U.S. Population: 106,021,537.
- On August 18, 1920, the 19th Amendment to the U.S. Constitution is ratified giving women the right to vote.
- KDKA in Pittsburgh, PA, becomes the first radio station to offer regular broadcasts on November 2, 1920.
- Lila Bell and DeWitt Wallace begin publishing *Reader's Digest* in 1922.
- F. Scott Fitzgerald publishes *The Great Gatsby* in 1925.
- Tennessee school teacher John T. Scopes' trial for teaching Darwin's "Theory of Evolution" begins in July of 1925.
- A. A. Milne publishes his first collection of stories about the character Winnie-the-Pooh in 1926.
- Charles Lindbergh lands "Spirit of St. Louis" in Paris on May 21, 1927, successfully completing the first trans-Atlantic flight.
- Audiences see the first motion picture with sound *The Jazz Singer* in 1927.
- Ford Motor Company celebrates as the 15 millionth Model T rolls off its Highland Park, MI, assembly line on May 26, 1927.
- Stock market crashed on "Black Thursday" (October 24, 1929) leading to the Great Depression

Cost of living (source: U.S. Bureau of the Census, *Historical Statistics of the United States, Colonial Times to 1970, Bicentennial Edition, Part 2.*, Bureau of Labor Statistics, 2011).

Flour (5 pounds)	41 cents
Bread (1 pound)	12 cents
Bacon (1 pound)	52 cents
Butter (1 pound)	70 cents
Eggs (1 dozen)	68 cents
Milk (1/2 gallon)	33 cents
Potatoes (10 pounds)	63 cents
Coffee (1 pound)	47 cents
Sugar (5 pounds)	97 cents

This photo (circa 1930) was taken at a tent revival
similar to the one that preceded the formation of
Munford First of Assembly of God Church.
Photo Courtesy of Peggy (Pinner) Cox

This photo depicts Glen Springs Lake in 1919. The hotel can be seen in the top left of the photo. A skating rink and movie theater are depicted in the top right. Photo courtesy of "Tales of Tipton."

FLASHBACK

Revival at Glen Springs in 1928 and at Crosstown in 1929 as written by William A. Bridges

So Brother Harvey Wiseman and a young man came from Oklahoma, and they and Brother Raymond Wiseman and his wife started a revival on the ground where the old hotel building was at that time at Glen Springs, but for several nights the people would not come under the tent. That was something new for them in that part. But, one night someone brought a young man from Arkansas in something like a wheelchair because he was helpless. People had said that he could not live. But these poeple had faith for him, and Brother Raymond Wiseman asked the people to stand back and give this man room to walk. So when they anointed him with oil and prayed, he came out of that chair walking. So then the revival really began. As many will remember, 1928, or at least some will remember.

I went out a few times to that meeting, and when they closed, plans were made to have revival at Munford, and as many will remember, the tent was erected at CrossTown (i.e. between Munford and Atoka). So, Brother Raymond Wiseman said to me, "Now, my brother is going back to Oklahoma, and I need you to help me, so just quit your job and come help me. I will preach the day service, and you preach at night." Yes, we had service night and day back then. People loved God then and many were anxious to have what God had for them. "Yes, I know it is different now, so many have lost all desire for God. It is pitiful. Yes, very sad."

So I went home that night, but did not go to bed, but prayed the rest of the night and went to work next morning and told my boss I was quitting my job and was going to preach. It was then that he asked if I would work long enough to train someone to take my place. So I agreed, and did work a few days longer.

We started the meeting already at CrossTown, and as I said, services lasted all night many times back then, so we would preach and pray all night and then I would work nine hours on my job, so I did not go to bed for several nights. But, God was blessing and I don't remember if I even got sleepy. This was in the summer of 1928.

This was my first meeting, and no doubt I made many mistakes, but God was good to us. Many souls prayed through, and several bodies were healed, Thank God. This meeting continued until the weather got cool so we took the tent down and began to have our regular church services in the home of Brother and Sister Millican's at Munford, continuing there until the church-building was ready, which was March 1st 1929.

- 13 -

Oh, God is so good to us. PRAISE GOD! Now, in the summer of 1929 we had another meeting at CrossTown, with Brother R. L. Wilkerson doing the preaching, and God did bless. The Spirit of revival continued, and in the summer of 1930 we had another meeting at the same place with Sister Irene Travis doing the preaching. God was yet blessing.

Church History as written in Stones by the River: A History of
the Tennessee District of the Assemblies of God in 1975
by J. Samuel Rasnake

Chapter XI

THE RIPLEY SECTION

The Ripley Section of the Tennessee District contained
twenty-three churches. Munford and four others were pio-
neered in the late twenties. Approximately seven churches
were opened in the 1930's — most of them in brush arbors.
Four were established in the 1940's. Two were started in the
1950's, and two began in the sixties. Brighton, Alamo, South
Tipton, and Henning started in the 1970's.

Munford — First Assembly. Raymond Wiseman, while in a
sanatorium with the last stages of tuberculosis, prayed for
God to spare his life long enough for his family to be saved
and build a church. In 1928 he brought a tent to Glenn
Springs, a health resort. Wiseman preached every night with
only a few in attendance. The Wisemans lived on blackberries
and bread. After three weeks of uneventful revival a young
man (so weak he had to be turned in a sheet) was carried to
the tent on a stretcher. After the evangelists prayed, God
raised him up.

The healing triggered a tremendous revival that continued
for four months. The tent was moved to Crosstown where
thousands gathered for the services. They roped off a large
area to keep spectators from crowding into the altars where
people were saved and filled with the Spirit. Someone erected
a dance hall across the street from the tent and night after
night, a band played outside. However, the dance hall went
out of business and the revival continued. A man running
from God started to board a bus, but changed his mind and
returned to the tent. He fell on the ground praying and beating the earth with his fists. God saved him two hours later,
but by that time he had dug a large hole in the ground. Hickman set the group in order in the home of Emery Pinner in
February, 1929, and the following were charter members:

E. H. and Mrs. Pinner, C. R. Farbess, C. R. Demery, R. H. Delancey, C. L. Burlison, T. H. Sylvestor, Russell Belk, T. M. and Mrs. Millican, W. A. Bridges, F. D. Wiseman, E. B. Carter, R. F. and Mrs. Wiseman, William Wiseman, Mrs. C. D. Demery, Mrs. C. P. Farbess, Mrs. T. L. Demery, Mrs. C. R. Pickard, Mrs. C. M. Burlison, Gladys Wiseman, Mrs. J. R. Adkison, Mrs. M. L. Jackson, Victoria Gillihan, Josephine Burlison, Alberta Smith, Lillian Wiseman, Helen Wiseman, Sarah Millican, and Gladys Millican.

The fourth district council convened in a tent at Crosstown near Munford with E. S. Williams as the speaker in 1929. During one of the altar services Maggie Valentine fell under the power of God. A flame of fire, visible to those praying in the altar, played over her face. She was filled with the Holy Spirit and commenced speaking with other tongues.

Following the council, services were conducted in the different homes until a church was built. The congregation raised cotton to pay for the building, and on December 24, 1929, the women and children pulled the cotton stalks as the men dug the foundation. A short time after its completion, the new building was drenched with coal oil and burned, so they were forced to resume the use of a tent.

Oliver Vine supervised the erection of the second building. That church also burned and the congregation worshiped in the different churches in town until they could rebuild. Most of the time they met in the Presbyterian Church. Melvin McBride was construction overseer of the third and present plant.

The following were members of the official board: Bill Williams, Paul Pickard, Thurston Starnes, Bill Greathouse, John Moore, and J. T. Forbess. The First Assembly's pastors were:

R. F. Wiseman, William Bridges, Brother Anderson, Brother Foshee, Brother Firkins, Brother Findley, Brother Berryhill, R. L. Wilkerson, Brother Salyers, Eluis King, W. E. Lindsey, Claude McKeel, T. J. Lemons, Paul McKeel, George Preslar, Brother Gladney, Earl Pritchard, E. R. Driver, C. M. Hicks, and the present pastor, Wayne Bradley.

There were 262 enrolled in the Sunday school, and the church gave more than $400 per month to twenty-eight missionaries in 1972. The present property is valued at more than $250,000.[1]

This is not law, only a suggestion. This may be adopted as it stands, or may be modified to meet the needs of any particular case. Pastors, and deacons should be men filled with the Holy Ghost.

CHURCH SET IN ORDER

Record of the Assembly of God at..............MUNFORD, TENNESSEE.

Date..............................FEBRUARY 3rd, 1929.

We, whose names appear upon the assembly roster, under above date, believing ourselves to be members of the General Assembly and Church of the first-born, whose names are written in heaven (Heb. 12:33), and after due deliberation and consideration of the constitution of the General Council of the Assemblies of God, adopted at Hot Springs, Ark., April 1 to 10, 1914, for the purpose of the promulgation and furtherance of the Gospel of Christ, our Lord, do hereby adopt

the same faith and recognize ourselves as an Assembly of God at MUNFORD, TENNESSEE.

and by the name of..............THE ASSEMBLY OF GOD, MUNFORD, TENNESSEE.

in co-operative fellowship with the General Council of the Assemblies of God (Incorporated), with headquarters and general offices at Springfield, Mo., in co-operation with the District Council; and we adopt the following as to membership, officers, and business meetings:

ARTICLE I.
MEMBERSHIP

1. Any person born of the Spirit (John 3:5) and who is living a consistent Christian life and who is in co-operative fellowship with our testimony, and who shall contribute according to his ability to the support of the church, may become an active member .... to any member of the official board, which shall, upon .... provide ....
3. .... themselves from regular services for the period of six consecutive months, or who may be under charges, shall not be considered in the legal voting membership of the Assembly.

ARTICLE II.
GOVERNMENT AND OFFICIAL FUNCTIONS

1. There shall be a board of deacons of not less than three and not more than seven members.
2. The board of deacons shall act as trustees and custodians of the church property.
3. There shall be a pastor, secretary, and treasurer.
4. The initiative shall be the right and privilege of all members of the church in good standing.
5. All standing committees shall be auxiliary and subject to the official board, consisting of pastor and deacons.

ARTICLE III.
ELECTIONS AND VACANCIES
THE PASTOR

(a) The pastor shall be chosen by the Assembly at the annual business meeting or at a special business meeting called for that purpose, and shall be considered elected to the office by a two-thirds majority vote of members present.
(b) The term of pastor's office shall be for a period of one year, or for an indefinite period as may be decided upon by the assembly at the time of election.
(c) A vacancy in the pastorate shall be supplied under the supervision of the Board of Deacons until a pastor is elected.
(d) In case at any time a situation should arise where, due to unscriptural conduct, change of doctrinal views, or inefficiency, a pastor can no longer serve the Assembly acceptably, it shall be the duty of the official board, upon exercise of the right of initiative by the Assembly, to call a special meeting of the Assembly, duly announced at two consecutive Sunday services. By a two-thirds majority vote of the legal voting membership present at such a meeting, the pastor's office may be declared vacant.
(e) Such action on the part of an assembly is not to be considered as affecting the standing of the pastor with the General Council fellowship.

DUTIES OF THE PASTOR

(a) The pastor shall be considered as the spiritual overseer of the assembly and all church activities. He shall be Chairman of the Board of Deacons and ex-officio member of all committees.
(b) The pastor shall be responsible for all the spiritual services, and shall have the oversight in arranging for special services, conventions, etc. No person shall be invited to speak or preach in the assembly unless by an understanding and in full harmony with the pastor's wishes.
(c) The pastor shall have the oversight of all visitation work, and may appoint others to assist him in this work.

(d) In the event of his absence, the pastor with the Board of Deacons, shall appoint some one to preside at business sessions, or to take charge of church services.

(e) The Young People's Society shall be recognized as a department of the church work and shall be under the supervision of the pastor.

ARTICLE IV.

BOARD OF DEACONS

(a) The Board of Deacons shall be elected by the Assembly at the annual election of officials, which shall take place the last day of the year, or at a time agreed upon.

(b) Vacancies on the Board of Deacons shall be filled by action of the Assembly at its annual, or quarterly meetings, or a special meeting called for that purpose.

(c) Vacancies in any office in the church may be declared by action of the Assembly whenever an incumbent has disqualified himself by unscriptural conduct, by a spirit of insubordination, or by a change of belief contrary to the articles of "Faith" herein, according to the plan outlined above in case of the pastor.

DUTIES OF THE DEACONS

(a) The deacons shall act in an advisory capacity with the pastor in all matters pertaining to the church in its spiritual life and in the administration of its ordinances. They shall act when required in the examination of applicants for membership, and also in the administration of the discipline of the church.

(b) The Board of Deacons, acting as trustees, shall have the oversight of all property and business matters of the church. They shall control and conduct the same in a business-like manner for the promotion of the purposes of the church as set forth in its regulations.

(c) All matters of church government shall be carried on by the official board except in matters affecting the entire body. In such cases they shall pass as recommendations to the Assembly for ratification.

ARTICLE V.

Business Meetings of the Assembly: We agree that there shall be a business meeting of the assembly every three months; every month if the assembly so desires. Also the pastor or deacons by majority agreement may call a business meeting at any time upon due notice, for the purpose of a closer co-operation in the local body. Such special business meetings of the assembly must be previously announced from the platform at a regular service, and when so called, a record shall be kept of all business transacted, the same as of the regular business meetings.

This meeting was called to order by SUPT. A. T. HICKMAN

ROBERT DELANCY ....was elected................

then proceeded to the signing of the roster, and those whose names appear under the above date on our church book are charter members of the assembly. The above articles were adopted. (Elect deacons only when you have proper material for same.)

R. E. WISEMAN ACTING AS PASTOR ....was elected as pastor.

T. M. MILLICAN ....was elected as secretary.

E. H. PINNER, O. R. FORBESS ....was elected as deacon.

O. D. DEMERY, AND R. H. DELANCY ....was elected as deacon.

C. L. BURLISON ....was elected as deacon.

We certify to the above as being correct.

Number of members ....31....
Use reverse side for names of Charter Members.

................*A. T. Hickman*................
Chairman.

Street Address. *P. O. Box 111 Mil*

................*Robert Delancy*................
Secretary.

Street Address. *Munford Tenn*

DUPLICATE

The

Executive Office

Ceneral Council · Assemblies of God

E. S. WILLIAMS, General Superintendent   FRED VOGLER, Ass't General Superintendent   J. R. FLOWER, General Secretary

336 W. PACIFIC STREET
SPRINGFIELD, MISSOURI

April 2, 1929

A VOLUNTARY COOP-
ERATIVE FELLOWSHIP
DEVOTED TO THE
PROPAGATION OF THE
GOSPEL OF JESUS
CHRIST IN THE
WHOLE WORLD.

THIRTY-FIVE DISTRICT
COUNCILS IN THE
UNITED STATES OF
AMERICA.

4,000 CHURCHES
MEMBERSHIP OF
200,000

FOREIGN MISSIONS
DEPARTMENT
42 MISSION FIELDS
380 MISSIONARIES

CENTRAL BIBLE
INSTITUTE
TRAINING SCHOOL FOR
MINISTERS AND
MISSIONARIES.
ACCOMMODATION FOR
300 STUDENTS

GOSPEL PUBLISHING
HOUSE
PENTECOSTAL EVAN-
GEL (WEEKLY)
CIRCULATION
OF 70,000

CHRIST'S AMBASSA-
DORS HERALD
(MONTHLY)

SUNDAY SCHOOL PUB-
LICATIONS AND
SUPPLIES.

The Assembly of God

Munford, Tennessee

T. M. Millican, Sec'y.

Greetings in the Name of Jesus!

In view of the action taken by your assembly at the meeting held February 3rd, 1929, copy of the Minutes having been received in this office, we hereby officially recognize the Assembly at Numford, Tennessee, as one of the local assemblies in co-operative fellowship with the General Council, Assemblies of God.

It is to be understood that this action on the part of the assembly, with this accompanying official recognition, gives to the local assembly the right of representation in all General Council meetings, and it is urged that the assembly send their pastor and one delegate to such General Council meetings to represent the local Assembly.

May the Lord bless and prosper you in Him.

Secretary of the General Council
Assemblies of God

This letter to be attached to and become a part of your assembly records.

Certificate of Affiliation

The General Council of the Assemblies of God

This is to Certify that

First Assembly of God
Munford, Tennessee

is hereby officially recognized as a church affiliated with
The General Council of the Assemblies of God, with all the privileges
and responsibilities as provided by the constitution and bylaws
of its district council and The General Council of the Assemblies of God.

Given this __2nd__ day of __April__ in the year of our Lord __1929__

General Superintendent

General Secretary

LICENSE TO PREACH

ISSUED BY THE

Tennessee District Council of the Assemblies of God

This Certifies that M*r.* ~~Raymon Wiser~~

of ~~Munford~~ State of ~~Tennessee~~

being a member of the general assembly of God (Heb. 12:23), having been divinely called according to the Word of God and in fellowship with the above District Council of the ASSEMBLIES OF God, is hereby given LICENSE TO PREACH; and we the undersigned, by fervent prayer, invoke the divine presence with blessings and power upon ~~him~~ and hereby recognize ~~him~~ as ~~a Minister~~ for one year from date, provided ~~he~~ remains in fellowship with the Assemblies of God, and maintains a Godly life and a scriptural standard in teaching.

Given This *30th* day of *Sept* 192*5*, A. D.

~~J. A. Smith~~

District Superintendent

~~W. G. Epps~~

District Secretary

To be renewed annually at each Council meeting.

16

Photos of Mr. and Mrs. William A. Bridges
Second Pastor at Munford Assembly of God.
He also assisted Pastor Wiseman at the Crosstown Revival in 1929.
Photo excerpt from *The Amazing Grace of God in the Life of
Bro. William A. Bridges*

Bro. & Sis. WILLIAM A. BRIDGES

BROTHER BRIDGES ON THE GO
WITH THE GOSPEL

Photos of Mr. and Mrs. Emery Pinner
Thirty one charter members set the church in order in their home on
February 3, 1929.
Parents of Marshall Pinner.
Grandparents of Martha Watkins, Peggy Cox, Dotty Rice and
Patricia Murphy.

This letter was sent in response to the revival, warning leaders not to build the church in the Munford community. The letter was re-written by Virginia Robertson, daughter of Raymond Wiseman (see next page).

Memphis, Tenn.
Nov. 10th, 1925.

Dear Sir:

We have been informed of the trouble you are disturbing out at Munford. We are peacemakers ourselves for the State of Tennessee. We have your history and now we will give you until Wednesday morning to leave the State to keep trouble down.

We have never seen you and you won't see us if you take us at our word, but if not, you will see us.

The Citizens of Munford have been here two times and they tell us you have torn their community all to pieces. There are five homes done up, so take us at our word.

If we have to come to the Church you are building we will protect our children and our daughters, but if so, you will see us.

Yours truly,

T H E - K . K

[box] 6 FEET

Re-written on other side. By Virginia Robertson, daughter of Raymond Wiseman

Letter re-written by Virginia Robertson,
daughter of Raymond Wiseman.

Memphis, Tenn.
Nov. 10th, 1928

Mr. Raymond Wiseman
Millington, Tennessee

Dear Sir,

We have been informed of the trouble you are disturbing out at Munford. We are peacemakers ourselves for the State of Tennessee. We have your history and now we will give you until Wednesday morning to leave the State to keep trouble down.

We have never seen you and you won't see us if you take us at our word, but if not, you will feel us.

The citizens of Munford have been here two times and they tell us you have torn their community all to pieces. There are five homes done up, so take us at our word.

In regards to the church you are getting built it must not go up because we will protect our state and don't let us have to come out. If so you will regret it.

Yours Truly

A letter signed by "Citizens of Munford"

Letter retyped for clarity

Mr. Raymond Wiseman:

We the undersigned agreed to notify you not to stick your head in our town any more as we are having too much trouble that you are causing. This church must not go up in this place.

Instead of it being a peace maker it is a Hell raiser and we don't need it or you either in this Town and don't aim to have it or you either, so to save trouble you had better take this warning.

Citizens of Munford

In August of 1929 The Tennesse District Council of the
Assemblies of God held a meeting in Munford.
These minutes are provided courtesy of Gladys M. Valentine.

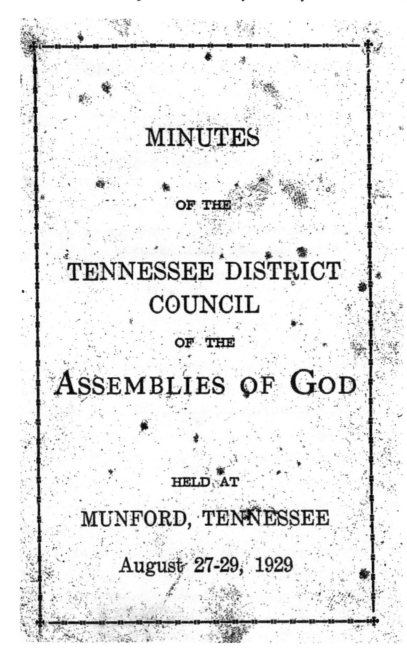

MINUTES

OF THE

TENNESSEE DISTRICT COUNCIL

OF THE

ASSEMBLIES OF GOD

HELD AT

MUNFORD, TENNESSEE

August 27-29, 1929

Tennessee District Council

OF THE

General Council

ASSEMBLIES OF GOD

—o—

OFFICERS

I. A. SMITH................................District Supt.
Memphis, Tenn., 1405 Aste St.

W. A. SPAIN.....Secretary and Treasurer
Milan, Tenn., Route 4

—o—

DISTRICT PRESBYTERS

R. L. WILKERSON.......Knoxville, Tenn.
1515 Madine Street

A. T. ABBOTT.................Greenville, S. C.
13 Wallace Street

T. B. Carter...................Memphis, Tenn.
1310 McMillan Street

—o—

DISTRICT PRESBYTERS

The Fourth Annual Session of the Tennessee District Council of the Assemblies of God convened at Munford, Tennessee, August 27-29, 1929, with the assembly of God at 10 a. m.

The Council opened with song and prayer, with J. R. Evans, secretary of the General Council, in the chair. At this time Bro. Evans brought a wonderful message which was greatly enjoyed by all, after which the Council adjourned to meet at 2:00 p. m.

AFTERNOON SESSION

After song and prayer, with Secretary J. R. Evans in the chair, we proceeded with business.

Resolutions Committee—R. L. Wilkerson, W. N. Mills and George Prebar.

Credentials Committee—A. T. Abbott, J. A. Smith and T. B. Carter.

Program Committee—W. A. Spain, J. A. Smith, William A. Bridges.

Field reports were heard at this time. Many of the brethren gave in reports of their work as to how the Lord had blessed their labor in the way of saving souls and healing the sick, for which we all praised the Lord. Evangelist William F. A. Griske of Los Angeles, Calif., gave an interesting talk, which was enjoyed by all. Council adjourned.

The evening service drew a vast multitude of people. Rev. J. R. Evans brought the evening message. Many responded to the altar call and a number prayed their way through to victory.

WEDNESDAY MORNING

Morning session opened with song and prayer, with Rev. A. T. Abbott reading a portion of the 19th chapter of Luke and II Cor. 5, after which we proceeded with business.

The secretary and treasurer read his report for the year ending September 1, which was adopted. Minutes of the previous session were read and adopted—whereas there was some money left in the treasury that, according to our plan, belonged to the superintendent, A. T. Hickman. After discussing the matter, there was a motion made and carried that this money

be retained in the treasury of the District Council. Council adjourned to meet at 2:00 p. m.

WEDNESDAY EVENING

Council opened with song and prayer, after which we proceeded with the election of officers. J. A. Smith was elected district superintendent; W. A. Spain was re-elected secretary and treasurer; A. T. Abbott, R. L. Wilkerson and T. B. Carter were elected Presbyters.

REPORT OF RESOLUTION COMMITTEE

Because of the traveling and other expenses connected with the office of district superintendent, we recommend that one-half of all ministers' tithes and one-half of home missions fund be given to the district superintendent, that he may properly superintend the work.

As the eastern division of the Tennessee District Council is several hundred miles away from the work of the western division it is very difficult for the ministers and delegates from either division to attend fellowship meetings held in the other division. We, the brethren of the eastern division, ask the District Council to subdivide the district into two divisions, eastern and western, and that the district presbytery shall represent the district superintendent in business, that is of such nature that Presbyters can take care of; also to have fellowship meeting separate from western division.

Whereas it is the desire of the brethren of the western Carolinas to be affiliated with the Tennessee District, be it resolved that we recognize them as a part of the Tennessee district until such time that they themselves become a district.

Whereas as there is some expense attached to the renewing of licenses, be it resolved that all of the licentiated send one dollar to the secretary for their renewals.

DUTIES OF THE DISTRICT SUPT.

(1) To preside at all meetings of the District Council.

(2) To be head of the district office and to supervise all the work of the district Presbyters in the interviews between sessions of the District Council.

(3) To superintend the work on the field and to encourage Bible and missionary conventions.

(4) To perform any other function usual and customary as presiding officers and such as may be directed by the district Presbyters.

DUTIES OF SECRETARY-TREASURER

(1) He shall keep a true record of all the proceedings of the District Council meetings and of all business transacted at all fellowship and Presbyteral meetings.

(2) He shall act as treasurer of the district Council receiving all home missionary offerings for the work of the district and shall pay the same out as directed by the Presbytery or by the Council.

(3) He shall have the minutes of the District Council meeting printed after the same has been duly edited and approved by the district officers.

DUTIES OF DISTRICT PRESBYTERS

(1) The district Presbyters shall act as general representatives and shall co-operate with the superintendent and secretary and ministers of the district in the interest of peace and progress of the entire fellowship.

It was moved and carried that we have the fellowship meetings in the Western division every fifth Sunday and that we have the fellow-

ship meetings in the eastern division the first Sunday in the month that the fifth Sunday occurs in.

It was moved and carried that we urge all of the pastors to give their assemblies a chance to contribute to the world-wide mission plan once a month.

It was moved and carried that we have our next District Council at Milan, Tennessee, September 3-5, 1930.

REPORT OF CREDENTIALS COMMITTEE

We, the Credentials Committee, submit the following names:

A. L. Chadwick for ordination; Bro. J. R. Evans had charge of the ordination service.

For license: E. McFarland, Mrs. Mattie Antwine, John Hopper, Peter J. Lunatia, Robert H. Delaney, Clarence L. Osburn, William A. Bridges, R. T. Wiseman, Mrs. Myrtle Reed.

VOTE OF THANKS

It was moved and carried that we give a vote of thanks to Pastor William A Bridges and his assembly for their hospitality rendered during the Council sessions. Council adjourned at 5. p. m.

LIST OF ORDAINED MINISTERS

Abbott, A. T., Greenville, S. C., 13th Wallace street.

Carter, T. B., Memphis, Tenn., 1310 McMillan street

Daniels, Mrs. M. E., Franklin, Tenn., Route 2

Gibbs, E. H., Knoxville, Tenn., 207 Damson Ave

Kennedy, A. J., Kingsport, Tenn., Route No. 2, box 259.

Mills, W. N., Dyersburg, Tenn.

Minutes of the Tennessee District Council of the Assemblies of God
(continued)

O'Bryan, T. R., Marion, Ky.

O'Donniley, W. H. Hurricane Mills, Tenn.

Presler, George, Dyer Tenn.

Rodgers, H. G., Bemis, Tenn.

Smith, J. A., Memphis, Tenn., 1405 Aste street.

Sullivan, Mrs. Percie, Harris, Tenn.

Spain, W. A., Milan, Tenn., Route 4.

Westbrook, J. L., Gadsden, Tenn.

Wilkerson, R. L., Knoxville, Tenn., 1515 Madin street.

Chadwick, A. L., Greenville, S. C., 13 Wallace street.

Walter B. Jessup, pastor Assembly of God, Memphis, Tenn., 289 California street.

LICENTIATES

Antwine, Mrs. Mattie, Bells, Tenn., Route 2.

Bridges, William A., Munford, Tenn.

Burkett, William H., Trenton, Tenn., 403 Factory street.

Delaney, Robert H., Munford, Tenn.

Hopper, John, Gadsden, Tenn.

Lunatia, Peter J., Memphis, Tenn., 905 Faxon street.

McFarland, E., Bradford, Tenn.

Osborne, Clarence L., Drummond, Tenn.

Reed, Mrs. Myrtle, Dyer, Tenn., Route 3.

Wiseman, R. T., Munford, Tenn.

A Statement of Fundamental Truths Approved by the General Council of the Assemblies of God—October 2 to 7, 1916.

—o—

According to our Constitution we have the right to approve of all Scriptural truth. The Bible is our all-sufficient rule for faith and practice. Hence this Statement of Fundamental Truths is not intended as a creed for the Church, nor as a basis of fellowship among Christians, but only as a basis of unity for the ministry alone (i. e., that we all speak the same thing, 1 Cor. 1:10, Acts 2:42). The human phraseology employed in such statement is not inspired nor contended for, but the truth set forth in such phraseology is held to be essential to a full Gospel ministry. No claim is made that it contains all truth in the Bible, only that it covers our present needs as to these fundamental matters.

1. THE SCRIPTURES INSPIRED

The Bible is the inspired Word of God, a revelation from God to man, the infallible rule of faith and conduct, and is superior to conscience and reason, but not contrary to reason (2 Tim. 3:15,16; 1 Pet. 2:2).

2. THE ONE TRUE GOD

The one true God has revealed Himself as the eternally self-existent, self-reveald "I AM;" and has further revealed Himself as embodying the principles of relationship and association, i. e., as Father, Son and Holy Ghost (Deut. 6:4; Mark 12:29; Isa. 43.10,11; Matt. 28:19).

Minutes of the Tennessee District Council of the Assemblies of God
(continued)

3. MAN, HIS FALL AND REDEMPTION

Man was created good and upright; for God said, "Let us make man in Our image and in Our likeness." But man, by voluntary transgression, fell, and his only hope of redemption is in Jesus Christ, the Son of God (Gen. 1:26-31; 3:17; Rom. 5:12-21).

4. THE SALVATION OF MAN

(a) Conditions to Salvation.

The grace of God that brings salvation to all men has appeared through the preaching of repentance toward God and faith toward the Lord Jesus Christ; whereupon man is saved by the washing of regeneration and renewing of the Holy Ghost, and, (having been justified by grace through faith, he becomes an heir of God according to the hope of eternal life (Titus 2:11; Romans 10:13-15; Luke 24:47; Titus 3:5-7).

(b) The Evidence of Salvation.

The inward evidence, to the believer of his salvation, is the direct witness of the Spirit (Rom. 8:16). The outward evidence to all men is a life of righteousness and true holiness (Luke 1:73,75; Titus 2:12-14); the fruit of the Spirit (Gal. 5:22); and brotherly love (John 13:35; Heb. 13:1; 1 John 3:14).

5. BAPTISM IN WATER

The ordinance of Baptism by a burial with Christ should be observed as commanded in the Scriptures, by all who have really repented and in their hearts have truly believed on Christ as Savior and Lord. In so doing, they have the body washed in pure water as an outward symbol of cleansing while their heart has already been sprinkled with the blood of Christ as an inner cleansing. Thus they declare to the world that they have died with Jesus and that they have also been raised with Him to walk in newness of life (Matt. 28:19; Acts 10:47,48; Rom. 6:4; Acts 20:21; Heb. 10:22).

6. THE LORD'S SUPPER

The Lord's Supper, consisting of the elements, bread and the fruit of the vine, is the symbol expressing our sharing the divine nature of our Lord Jesus Christ (2 Pet. 1:4); a memorial of His suffering and death (1 Cor. 11:26); and a prophecy of His second coming (1 Cor. 11:26); and is enjoined on all believers "until He comes."

7. THE PROMISE OF THE FATHER

All believers are entitled to, and shall ardently expect, and earnestly seek the promise of the Father, the baptism in the Holy Ghost and fire, according to the command of our Lord Jesus Christ. This was the normal experience of all in the early Christian Church. With it comes the enduement of power for life and service, the bestowment of the gifts and their uses in the work of the ministry (Luke 24:49; Acts 1:4; 1:8, 1 Cor. 12:1-31).

8. THE FULL CONSUMATION OF THE BAPTISM IN THE HOLY GHOST

The full consummation of the baptism of believers in the Holy Ghost is indicated by the initial physical sign of speaking with other tongues as the Spirit of God gives them utterance (Acts 2:4). This wonderful experience is distinct from and subsequent to the experience of the new birth (Acts 10:44-46; 11:14-16; 15:7-9). The speaking in tongues in this instance is the same in essence as the gift of tongues (1 Cor. 12:4-10-28), but different in purpose and use.

9. ENTIRE SANTIFICATION THE GOAL OF ALL BELIEVERS

The Scriptures teach a life of holiness without which no man shall see the Lord. By the power of the Holy Ghost we are able to obey the command, "Be ye holy, for I am holy." Entire sanctification is the will of God for all believers.

and should be earnestly pursued by walking in obedience to God's word (Heb. 12:14; 1 Peter 1:15, 16; 1 Thess. 5:23, 24; I John 2:6).

10. THE CHURCH A LIVING ORGANISM

The Church is a living organism; a living body; yea the body of Christ; a habitation of God through the spirit, with divine appointments for the fulfillment of her great commission. Every true believer and every true local assembly are integral parts of the General Assembly and Church of the First born, written in heaven (Eph. 1:22, 23; 2:22, Heb. 12:23).

11. THE MINISTRY AND EVANGELISM

A divinely called and Scripturally ordained ministry is the command of the Lord for the evangelism of the world and the chief concern of the Church (Mark 16:15-20; Eph.4:11-13)

12. DIVINE HEALING

Deliverance from sickness is provided for in the atonement, and is the privilege of all believers (Isa. 53:4, 5; Matt. 8:16, 17).

13. THE BLESSED HOPE

The Resurrection of those who have fallen asleep in Christ, the rapture of believers which are alive and remain, and the translation of the true church, this is the blessed hope set before all believers (1 Thess. 4:16, 17; Rom. 8:23; Titus 2:13.)

14. THE IMMINENT COMING AND MILLENIAL REIGN OF JESUS

The premillennial and imminent coming of the Lord to gather His people unto Himself, and to judge the world in righteousness while reigning on the earth for a thousand years is the expectation of the true Church of Christ.

15. THE LAKE OF FIRE

The devil and his angels, the beast and false prophet, and whosoever is not found written in the Book of Life, the fearful and unbelieving, and abominable, and murderers and whoremongers, and sorcerers, and idolators and all liars shall be consigned to everlasting punishment in the lake which burneth with fire and brimstone, which is the second death (Rev. 19:20; Rev. 20:10:15).

16. THE NEW HEAVEN AND NEW EARTH

We look for new heavens and a new earth wherein dwelleth righteousness (2 Pet. 3:13; Rev. 21 and 22).

VIOLATIONS OF MINISTERIAL COURTESY

Resolved, That all discourteous conduct is disapproved and that all ministers are advised against interfering with others who may have charge of an assembly, whether it be by going in upon the work without consent of the one in charge or by such correspondence with the members of the assembly as will affect the influence of the leader. All correspondence which concerns the whole assembly, such as visiting that field, holding meetings, etc., should be addressed to the one in charge, not to private members. When there is no pastor, letters concerning the word should be addressed to the deacons or elders of the Assembly.

Any minister who so offends should be subjected to a Sricptural treatment as an offender, and it is recommended that it be given him by local authorities, or the District Council, or if there be none, by the Executive Presbytery of the General Council. Such matters will seriously affect the granting of annual Fellowship Certificates and may be the basis of their recall.

Ministers of the Gospel related to Charter Members	Charters
	Forbess
1- James + Joyce Belk	
2- Craig + Cindi Gregson	Millican
3 Robert + Jocie Delancy	Burlison + Del
4 Steve Good	Pickard
5- Brandon + Ashley Watkiss	Gladys M.
6- Stephen Pickard	Pickard, Demey
7- Gary Wilkes	Burlison
8- Bob + Mary Greathouse	Forbess
9. Bill + Janice Greathouse	Gladys Millican
10- Robert + Jocie Delancy son	Delancey
11 Cecil + Joyce Stapleton	Millican
12 Bill Cole	Forbess
13- Wilda + Robert Wright	Forbess
14. Tom Millican	Millican
15- James Mayer	Millican
16- Jethro Lindsey	
17- Dewey + Gracie Lindsey	Gilliham
18- Donny + Wife Baker	
19- Jimmy + " Baker	
20- Perry + Nancy Pittman	Bridges
21- Jennifer + Todd + Husband & Daughter	Atkison
22- Mervin Gross + Wife Blanch	Jackson
23- Ben + Maude Belk	Gilliham
24- Marshall + Kathryn Delashmit	Gilliham
25- Keithel + Joyce Boothe	Gilliham
26 Bessie + Emery Pinner	Pinner

The Early Days (1930-1939)

The founding members of the church wanted to serve in accordance with Acts 2:4, "And they were all filled with the Holy Ghost, and began to speak with other tongues, as the Spirit gave them utterance" (King James version of the Holy Bible). On November 28, 1931, they developed "Rules and advice for the church to be governed by at Munford, Tennessee." The rules reflected biblical practices common for that era including advice for all members to refrain from the use of tobacco, for sisters to dress modestly and not wear bobbed hair, and for only men to be elected as deacons serving as peace makers under the leadership of the pastor.

On February 20, 1935, the original church building was burned down. There were some who believed that those who sent the warning letters in 1928 were also responsible for the fire; however, there was little proof to confirm who committed the crime. Instead of dwelling on who was responsible for burning down the building, church leaders set about constructing a new building.

Music was part of the worship service as evidenced by photos from the 1930s. One of the more interesting photos includes a group of 24 people in front of the original church with three people holding guitars. Names for many of the people in the pictures are available thanks to the historical stewardship provided by Peggy (Pinner) Cox and Janice (Valentine) Greathouse (both of whom attended River of Life/Munford Assembly of God Church their entire lives).

One of the many blessings I had writing this book was interviewing Loree (Millican) Cole, who was 10 years old when the church was formed and has been a member of the church ever since. "My best memory would be of having church at my mother and daddy's house and at the Pinner home (before the first church building was finished)" (L. Cole, personal interview, May 3, 2013).

Ms. Cole also remembers the first church building. "There was a cotton patch, and we young kids went out and pulled up the cotton stalks to get ready for putting down the foundation. We had open windows in the summertime and people were standing outside (because they) couldn't get in that little church" (L. Cole, personal interview, May 3, 2013).

The young people also learned the importance of giving to those in need, even if it meant doing so in an unorthodox manner. For example, Dorothy (Valentine) Williams and Janice (Valentine) Greathouse shared a story about a time when their mother (Gladys Millican) received an unexpected charge to her account at the local grocery store. Apparently their mother's younger sisters, Sarah Millican and Loree (Millican) Cole decided they would buy groceries for a local family. They did this when they were young teenagers.

When Aunt Sarah and Aunt Loree were teenagers, they knew this family with little children who only had "gravy and biscuits to eat …and they just didn't think that was right because Grandma Millican, she always fixed a feast, I'm sure, at every meal. So mother (their older sister, Gladys Millican) had a charge account at this grocery store, and they went up there and charged some groceries to give to them. They took it upon themselves to bless the family at (their older sister's) expense," (Williams and Greathouse, personal interview, December 11, 2013).

This anecdote serves as a great example of how life lessons are more often caught than taught, especially lessons about serving others.

Historical events from the 1930s (source: U.S. Census Bureau)

- President of the United States: Herbert Hoover, Franklin Delano Roosevelt.
- U.S. Population: 123,202,624.
- 3M employee Richard Drew invents Scotch Brand Cellulose Tape in 1930. Today, it is widely known simply as "Scotch Tape."
- The Mickey Mouse comic strip debuts in the January 13, 1930, edition of the *New York Mirror*.
- Democrat Franklin D. Roosevelt defeats incumbent Republican Herbert Hoover in the 1932 election.
- The Boulder Dam (today known as "Hoover Dam") is completed two years ahead of schedule on March 1, 1936.
- Jesse Owens wins four gold medals during the 1936 Summer Olympics.
- Ty Cobb, Walter Johnson, Christy Mathewson, Babe Ruth, and Honus Wagner become the first inductees into the National Baseball Hall of Fame in 1936.
- The German airship Hindenburg is destroyed while attempting to land at the Lakehurst Naval Air Station on May 6, 1937.
- American aviation pioneer Amelia Earhart disappears over the Pacific Ocean while attempting to circumnavigate the globe, July 2, 1937.
- *Superman* debuts in Action Comics #1 in June 1938.
- *Gone with the Wind* wins the Academy Award for "Best Picture" in 1939.

Cost of living (source: U.S. Bureau of the Census, *Historical Statistics of the United States, Colonial Times to 1970, Bicentennial Edition, Part 2.*, Bureau of Labor Statistics, 201133)

Flour (5 pounds)	23 cents
Bread (1 pound)	9 cents
Round Steak (1 pound)	43 cents
Bacon (1 pound)	43 cents
Butter (1 pound)	47 cents
Eggs (1 dozen)	45 cents
Milk (1/2 gallon)	28 cents
Oranges (1 dozen)	57 cents
Potatoes (10 pounds)	36 cents
Coffee (1 pound)	40 cents
Sugar (5 pounds)	31 cents

Raymond F. Wiseman was the first pastor of Munford Assembly of God. William A. Bridges assumed the pastoral duties after Wiseman's death on March 27, 1930. Excerpt from *The Amazing Grace of God in the life of Bro. William A. Bridges.*

Oh, God is so good to us. PRAISE GOD! Now, in the summer of 1929 we had another meeting at CrossTown, with Brother R. L. Wilkerson doing the preaching, and God did bless. The Spirit of revival continued, and in the summer of 1930 we had another meeting at the same place with Sister Irene Travis doing the preaching. God was yet blessing.

Oh, GLORY HALLELUJAH. the blessings of God are so wonderful, but in this life we do have sorrow. For some reason, God chose to take one of His faithful servants home to be with Him. Yes, our dear Brother Raymond Wiseman was called to be with Jesus. But before he passed away, he told me that he had a dream or a vision and that he was in Heaven and could see his body lying in a casket in the church building, and that the Saints were mourning for him, but he wanted me to tell them "Don't mourn for me. I'm not there." The next few days he lived, I was with him and some of the saints. He would have us sing and pray and he would praise God saying, "This is wonderful". Yes, he died in the faith, and what he told me has been a real encouragement to me and especially when I am called to preach the funeral of someone who has died in the faith. Numbers 23:10; Psalms 23:4; 116:15; St. Luke 16:22; Romans 14:8; Philippians 1:21; the soul which is the conscious part of us does not go to the grave but to Paradise. Ecclesiastes 3:21; St. Luke 23:43? Revelation 2:7.

In this photo (circa 1930), members stand in front of the original church building. Photo courtesy of Peggy (Pinner) Cox.

1. Emery Pinner
2. Brother Ervin
3. C.D. (B. Jack) Demery
4. Willie Clay (Delancey) Adkison
5. Vadie Hanks
6. Ruth (Forbess) Starnes
7. Sister Ferkin
8. Brother Ferkin
9. Unknown
10. Letha Belk
11. Kate (Forbess) Millican
12. Hazel (Delancey) Burlison
13. Ms. Perry
14. Hattie (Forbess) Delancey
15. Ms. Busby
16. Ms. Ervin
17. Vick Gillihan
18. Mag (Laxton) Valentine
19. Chester Ruleman
20. Mr. Busby
21. Unknown
22. Unknown
23. Unknown
24. Clifton Valentine

In this photo (circa 1930), members stand in front of the original church building. Photo courtesy of Peggy (Pinner) Cox.

1. Cecil Belk
2. William Rhodes
3. Elton Valentine
4. Brother Ferkin
5. Wilma (Starnes) Lindsey
6. Theo Burlison
7. Lanelle (Bomar) Timbs
8. Chester Ruleman
9. Diane (Pickard) Goode
10. Edward Hanks
11. Dorothy (Starnes) Hanks
12. Virgil Bomar
13. Leon Campbell
14. Elvie Campbell
15. Loreen Belk
16. Hazel (Delancey) Burlison
17. Willie Clay (Delancey) Adkison
18. Doris (Dickerson) Williams
19. Sister Ferkin
20. Dorothy (Delashmit) Pinner
21. Unknown
22. Mary Helen Ruleman
23. Mary Ruth Fite
24. Marshall Pinner

Pastor W.E. Lindsey (circa 1930).
Photo courtesy of Loree (Millican) Cole.

2- PASTOR. Rev. W.E. LINdSey

GRANdMA LiNdSey & siSTeR LiNdSey

1930's

William Rhodes, Edward Hanks, Marshall Pinner, Leon Campbell
(circa 1930)

On November 28, 1931, founders developed "Rules and advice for the church to be governed by." The original document was found in a "cash book," which was used to record business meeting notes, roster roll reports, and finances.

Rules and advice for the church to be governed by at Munford Tenn.

Passed Nov 28-3

1st) Resolve: That they have a born agai experience, And in fellow ship wit[h] Acts 2:4. Living holy lives and each member refrain from the us[e] of tobacco in any form 2 Cor 7:1 Isa 55:2

2) We advise our sisters to dress Modist as the scriptures teaches and not wear bobbed hair.

3) We recomend that our church elect only men according to scriptural qualification as their deacons, Relecting them each year. And that they cooperate with their pastor. They are to work under the pastor and be a peace maker in the church.

4) We advise our church to only ellect S.S Teachers that will love their class and will devote their time to it endevering to come every sunday, 5 Our S.S. Supt. is to be a sober spirit party

6 Our trustees are to be men with buisness qualities

7 Resolve: that a church Sect. and Tresury be elected to keep minutes of all buisness meeting and care for the fiance Reports.

6th) We recomend that the church storehouse system be adopted accoding to the scriptures for

Rules: and advice for the church to be governed by at Munford Tenn.

the tithe to be given in accordian to the scripture (Mal 3:10, Deut 14:22,23 Neh 10:37, 1 Cov 9: 9-14 for the purpose of caring for the pastor. We recomend that our pastor give the sect. a statement of what was given him and by who so the sect can gi a report once each month.

On November 28, 1931, founders elected officers. The original
document was found in a "cash book," which was used to record
business meeting notes, roster roll reports, and finances.

Officers elected. Nov. 28-1931

Sect.	Sister Wiseman			
Trustee	Bro Ben Belk			
"	Bro Beckett			
"	Bro Dick Wiseman			
"	Bro Byack Slimery			
"	Bro Ruleman			
S.S. Supt	Bro Pinner			
Deacons	Bro Ruleman			
"	Bro Pinner			
"	Bro Beckett			
S.S. Sect	Bro Mervin Gross			
S.S.Teachers	Sister Wiseman	Class no 5		
"	Sister Gladys Millican	Class no 2		
"	Sister Adkinson	Class no 4		
"	Sister Wilson	Class no 1		
"	Sister Anderson	Class no 3		
Bro.	chester Ruleman	Class no 6		

This is a list of church members from 1931-1936. The original document was found in a "cash book," which was used to record business meeting notes, roster roll reports, and finances.

Church Members — 1931   11

Formor buisness by Pastor Nov 28-51
Rastaru Roll.

Bro.	Byack, demury		
"	Percy Dixie oxo?		
Sister	Starnes Ruth		
Bro	Ruleman Chester		
Sister	Ruleman Hattie		
Bro	Mervin Gross ?		
Bro	dick Wiseman ?		
Sister	Wiseman pearl		
Sister	Josie Pickard		
Bro	Ben Belk ?		
Bro	Authur Belk		
Bro	Beckett J. L. inactive		
Sister	Beckett Alice inactive		
Sister	Gladys Millican Valentine		
Sister	Lena Millican		
Sister	Millican Kate		
Sister	C. P. Forbess		
Sister	Boman Macie		
Sister	Delashmight Susie ✓		
Sister	Cole Ila		
Sister	Ethel Moore comot		
Sister	Leona Wiseman		
Sister	Mary Helen Ruleman		
Bro	Pinner Emery		
Sister	Pinner Bessie		
Sister	Adkinson Willie Clay ✓		
Bro	Flanagin Ernest ? inactive		
Sister	Delaney Hattie deceased 1936		
Sister	Victora Gillahan (Deceased 1942)		
Sister	Lois Guthrie Deceased		
Sister	Cora Guthrie Deceased July 3, 1933		
Bro.	W. H. Guthrie deceased 1936		
Sister	Leather Belk Deceased Feb. 2, 1936		
Sister	Valentine Maggie		

Church members from 1931-1936 (continued).

Sister Evelyn Fite ✓

Bro. Henry Fite

Sister Burlison Mae — inactive

Bro. J. H. Rhodes

Sister Rachel Taliaferro

Sister Dorthy Starnes

Sister Wilma Starnes

Bro. Berry — inactive

Sister Berry — ?

Sister Patsy Duvall

Sister Linnie Moore

Sister Windbury Maud — away

" Windbury Maud — away

Sis. Jackson Lee — inactive

15 new members added

August 5, 1934

Bro. J. L. Belk deceased April 1936

" F. G. Busby

Sis. Hattie Busby

" Warren Busby

" Vera Busby

Sis. S. H. Holland — deceased

" Annie Sue Chapman

Bro. Woodrow Craig

Annie Mae Fite ? inactive

Dorothy Debastnit Pinner

Sis. C. D. Dennery

" Theo Gilliam — inactive

" Margret Ruth Fite ✓

" Frankie Sue Burlison Jr.

" 7 Annie Patterson

42

Church members from 1931-1936 (continued).

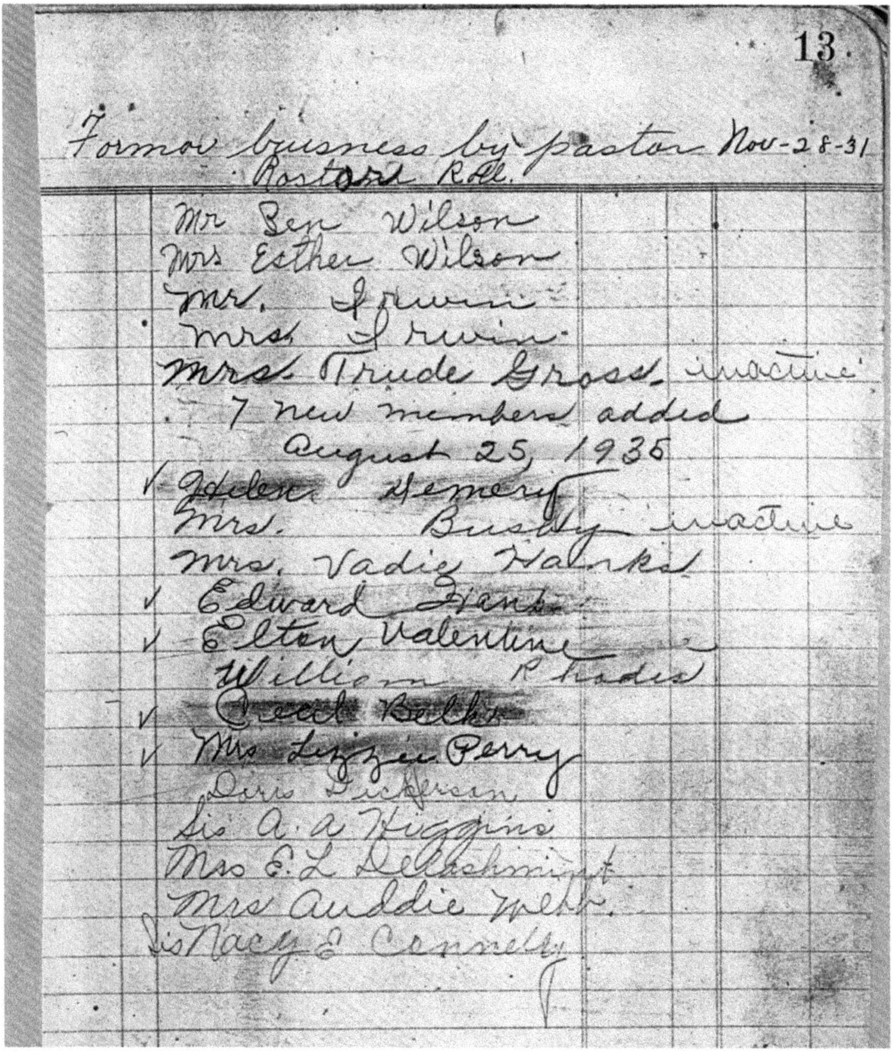

Formal business by pastor Nov-28-31
Pastor's Roll.

Mr Ben Wilson
Mrs Esther Wilson
Mr. Irwin
Mrs Irwin
Mrs Trude Gross — inactive
7 new members added
August 25, 1935
✓ Helen Hemery
Mrs. Busby — inactive
Mrs. Vadie Hanks
✓ Edward Hanks
✓ Elton Valentine
William Rhodes
✓ Cecil Belk
✓ Mrs Lizzie Perry
Dan Dickerson
Sis A. A. Higgins
Mrs E. L. Delashmiyt
Mrs Auddie Webb
Sis Macy E. Connelly

13

This is a list of collections and incidental expenses for November 1931. Total collections for the month were $14.95 in addition to tithes of $37.05. The original document was found in a "cash book," which was used to record business meeting notes, roster roll reports, and finances.

Collections for incerdential expenses
for month of Nov. 1931

Penny march	Nov. 1.		75
" "	Nov. 8		77
" "	" 15		63
" "	" 22		50
" "	" 29		30
Men collection for furniture	Nov 1.		45
" " " "	Nov 8		60
" " " "	Nov 15		30
" " " "	Nov 22		30
" " " "	Nov 29		35
Women collection for furniture	Oct 28	1	65
Women collection for furniture	Nov. 4	1	15
" " " "	Nov. 11	1	20
" " " "	Nov 18		70
" " " "	Nov 25		30
" " " "	Nov 25	6	00
Penny march for nov.		2	95
Mens bible class for Furniture		2	00
Ladies bible class for Furniture		10	00
Total collections		14	95
Paid on furniture		13	00
Paid on incedintial		2	57
Tithes		37	05

This is a list of "provisions for Brother Lindsey in 1933." The provisions included donations of food from families in the church. The original document was found in a "cash book," which was used to record business meeting notes, roster roll reports, and finances.

Provision for Bro Lindsey 1933

Date	Item	Qty/Price	Donor
Dec 26	29 lb meat	104 lb.	2.9
	5 lb sausage		
	1 bu turnips		sister Rulaman
Jan 10	1/2 bu potato sweet		Rulaman
	8 pounds soap		sister Rulaman
Jan 3	sugar	25¢	Wiseman
3	salt	5	Willa C.
3	baking pwd.	10	Willa C.
3	soap		sister Hanks
3	washing tab		Millican
3-6	cans cream	25¢	Starnes
3-1	box starch	5	Wilson
3-1 lb	butter	20	sister mu..
Jan 10	flour	50	Wiseman
10	rice	25	Millican
10	beans	25	Millican
10			
10	onions		Starnes
10	spagoti		Starnes
Jan	1 bu. Turnips		Rulaman
Jan 10	sugar	50	Mabel Denny
Jan 16	milk 2 cans	10	Millican
	salt	5	Millican
	soda	5	Millican
	lard 4 lbs.		Wiseman
Jan 24	oats		Starnes
	Potato		Bonar
	gallon peas		Owen

List of "provisions for Brother Lindsey in 1933" (continued).

Provisions for bro Lindsey 1933

Jan	24	molasses	5 0	Wiseman
"	24	cream 2 cans	1 5	Wiseman
"	24	flour	5 0	Millican
"	24	~~~~		
"	24	~~~~		
"	24	~~~~		
"	24	~~~~		
"	24	potats		Bro Ben Wilson
"	24	~~~~		
"	24	black pepper	1 0	Starnes
"	24	2 boxes oats	2 0	Starnes
"	24	2 boxes spagetti	1 0	Starnes
"	24	sugar 7 lbs.	3 5	Starnes
"	24	2 boxes starch	1 0	Starnes
"	27	s. potats 1 bu.		Delashmond
"	27	pop corn		Delashmond
"	27	1 gal molasses		Delashmond
"	27	Irish potats		Delashmond
"	27	lard 4 lb		Delashmond
"	27	peas		Delashmond
"	27	sugar		Delashmond
		1 .		~~Delashmond~~
"	29	1 doz eggs		Ruleman
Jan	31	1 can baking powd	1 0	Wiseman
	31	salt	1 5	Wiseman
	31	onions	1 0	Wiseman
	31	1 sack flour		Bro Ruleman
		1/2 gal of hominy		Sis Ruleman
		10 lb lard		Sis Ruleman

This is a list of "money paid out in 1936." The list also included "money taken in." Some of the expenses included $26.02 for missions (April – October) and lights $8.92 (April – September). Tithes recorded were $184.11. The original document was found in a "cash book," which was used to record business meeting notes, roster roll reports, and finances.

This is a "Roster Roll for July 25, 1937." Brother Claude McKeel is listed as the pastor. The original document was found in a "cash book," which was used to record business meeting notes, roster roll reports, and finances.

Faith and Perseverance (1940-1949)

"Church burned this morning. Special business meeting called by pastor at the parsonage." This was how the church secretary recorded one of the most devastating days in the church history on October 20, 1946. The record went on to show that there were seven members present who discussed, "whether or not the church should be built back where it was. Decided that we would use our present lot."

There are two observations about this single entry that consisted of just a partial page with less than 50 words. The first is the matter-of-fact manner in which the entry was made. No words of regret, sadness, or despair. Just the facts and a decision to rebuild. The second is gratitude that the church secretary, Gladys Valentine, had the presence of mind to record this in the ledger used to document the church business.

An important part of what happened in 1946 was the timing of the fire. According to eye witnesses, the fire started after a member of the church lit the basement stove to warm up the church. The basement is where the children would be later in the morning for Sunday School. According to Dorothy (Valentine) Williams, "I wouldn't be here if we had been in Sunday School (when the fire started)" (D. Williams personal interview, May 7, 2013).

Another important part of the 1946 fire was what happened after the church building burned down. The Munford Presbyterian Church members allowed the members of Munford Assembly of God to worship in the Presbyterian Church building on Sunday afternoons until the new Munford Assembly of God Church was rebuilt. According to Faye Ellis, "I remember we went to the Presbyterian Church. They opened their church for us to attend services there" (F. Ellis, personal interview, May 3, 2013). The Presbyterians also donated $1,000 to help with the rebuilding efforts. Many of the church members interviewed for this book continued to express gratitude for the outpouring of support from their fellow Christians from a different denomination, because they believe that the love shown by the members of Munford Presbyterian Church reflected the love of Christ.

Faye Ellis also shared her memories of church members coming together to rebuild, "I remember us young people chopping cotton and picking cotton to pay on that building, on the new building. We all wanted to do our part. Even the children wanted to do their part to help rebuild the church" (F. Ellis, personal interview, May 3, 2013).

Part of the research for this book was spent digging through church records which consisted of business meeting minutes, expense records, official correspondence, photos, and other documents in the church building and generously loaned by many members of the church. This book would not have been possible without the diligence of church secretaries like Gladys Valentine, Doris (Dickerson) Williams, Dorothy (Valentine) Williams, Janice (Valentine) Greathouse, Peggy (Pinner) Cox, and Jess and Ila Cole. Much of what is found in this and other chapters reflect the dedication of these servants along with other church families who shared their precious memories captured in photos, documents, and personal testimonies.

The book was also made possible through the time church members gave through personal interviews. One of the more-entertaining interviews was with Bill and Dorothy Williams. Bill is a World War II veteran, and he joined the church after his service in the Army Air Corps.

Bill described some of his early experiences in the church in the 1940s, "We (were) baptized in a pond out in the pasture…when he took me down I said, 'Boy, don't you turn me loose in this mess'" (B. Williams, personal interview, May 7, 2013). Readers of this book can appreciate how church members must have been grateful to have a baptismal as part of the church built in the 1940s.

Historical events from the 1940s (source: U.S. Census Bureau)

- Presidents of the United States: Franklin Delano Roosevelt and Harry S. Truman.
- U.S. Population: 132,164,569.
- Marvel Comics introduces superhero Captain America in March 1941.
- After approximately 14 years, carving at Mount Rushmore concludes in October 1941.
- Diarist Anne Frank and her family go into hiding in the "Achterhuis" on July 6, 1942, in Amsterdam.
- Walt Disney wins a 1943 Academy Award for his animated short film *Der Fuehrer's Face*.
- Band leader Alton Glenn Miller disappears while enroute to Paris, France, December 15, 1944.
- Department stores begin selling Tupperware® in 1946.
- Charles Yeager becomes the first man to break the sound barrier on October 14, 1947, flying the experimental Bell X-1 at Mach 1 at an altitude of 45,000 ft.
- NASCAR® holds its first modified stock car race in Daytona Beach, FL, in 1948.
- George Orwell publishes *Nineteen Eighty-Four* in 1949.

Cost of living (source: U.S. Bureau of the Census, *Historical Statistics of the United States, Colonial Times to 1970, Bicentennial Edition, Part 2.*, Bureau of Labor Statistics, 2011)

Flour (5 pounds)	22 cents
Bread (1 pound)	8 cents
Round Steak (1 pound)	36 cents
Bacon (1 pound)	27 cents
Butter (1 pound)	36 cents
Eggs (1 dozen)	33 cents
Milk (1/2 gallon)	26 cents
Oranges (1 dozen)	29 cents
Potatoes (10 pounds)	24 cents
Coffee (1 pound)	21 cents
Sugar (5 pounds)	26 cents

This photo was taken in the summer of 1946.
This is the second church building.
Photo courtesy of Bill and Dorothy (Valentine) Williams.

This photo was taken in 1948. It is the third church building, and this area of the church is used primarily by the youth group today. Photo courtesy of Bill and Dorothy (Valentine) Williams.

Former Pastors Claude and Paul McKeel. Claude served the church in the 1930s and Paul served in the 1940s.
Photo courtesy of Loree (Millican) Cole.

Reverend George Preslar, Pastor 1947-1951.
Photo courtesy of Bill and Dorothy (Valentine) Williams.

Church picnic held on July 4, 1947, on farm land worked by the
Valentine brothers. Photo courtesy of Bill Williams.

Wheel Barrow Race
Spencer & Loree Cole

Wheel Barrow Race
Charlie & Virginia Flo
Hansen

Photos courtesy of
Bill Williams

Church picnic held on July 4, 1947, on farm land worked by the Valentine brothers. Photo Courtesy of Bill & Dorothy Williams.

Church Picnic
Winners of Men's Cake Baking
Contest: W.J. Cole, Grady Layton
Spencer Cole

Photo Courtesy of
Bill & Dorothy Williams

Church picnic held on July 4, 1947, on farm land worked by the Valentine brothers. Attendees included Loree Cole, Elvie Campbell, Maggie Valentine, Elsie Garner, Macie Bomar, Willie Clay Adkison, Ruth Starnes, and R.C. Smith.
Photo courtesy of Bill and Dorothy (Valentine) Williams.

Church picnic held on July 4, 1947, on farm land worked by the Valentine brothers. Attendees included Doris Williams, Elizabeth (Lindsey) Cates, Diane Goode, Lilly Cole Wallis, and Grady Layton. Photo courtesy of Bill and Dorothy (Valentine) Williams.

Baptizing at Bishop's Pond in 1947 or 1948.
Photo courtesy of Bill Williams.

Business meeting held on the day the second church building burned on October 26, 1946.

Business meeting – Oct. 20, 1946
Church burned this morning.

Special business meeting called
by pastor at the parsonage
Those present,
Bro. Mc Keel.
Bro. Demery
Bro. Ruland
Bro. Higgins
Bro., White (Dist. Supt.)
Sis. Gladys Valentine
Bro. Thomas Gooder
Discussion on whether or not
the church should be built
back where it was.
Decided that we would use
our present lot.

Business meeting held on January 10, 1943, included elections for Church Secretary, Missionary Secretary, Sunday School Secretary and Treasurer, and Sunday School Superintendent.

Business meeting held Jan- 10 1943

Business meeting held Sun. morning Jan. 10,1943, was presided over by Rev. Lemon pastor. Names of active members of the church were read by church Sec. Mrs. Gladys Valentine Forty members were present - prayer was offered by all standing.

A finincial report was made by the Sec. + Treas. The record was accepted by the church.

It was agreed that the church Sec. keep a record of all the tithes.

Sis Ila Cole was elected as missionary Sec.

Sis. Doris Dickerson was re-elected as S.S. Sec. + Treas for one year.

Nominations for S.S. Supt. were made Bro pinner and Bro Bomar were nominated

prayer was offered by all standing.

Bro Bomar was re-elected as S.S. Supt.

Bro. pinner was re-elected as assistant S.S. Supt.

Rules and regulations concerning the deacons was read from the minutes by Rev. Lemons. ─── [Bro welch]

Business meeting held on January 10, 1943, (continued) included
elections for Deacons, Church Secretary, and Treasurer.

Rev. Lemons.
(Bowelsh)
    The office of one deacon was vacant.
The new deacon was to serve three years.
Nominations were made from the floor
in the following order { Bro Pinner
                                 Bro. Ruleman.
                                 Bro Welsh.
    Vote was taken by secret ballot.
Bro. Ruleman was elected as deacon for
3 yrs.
    Nominations were made from the
floor for church Secretary & Treas. in the
Continued on Page 16.

following order { Mrs Gladys Valentine
                      { Mr. E. H. Pinner
                      { Mr. Edward Hanks.
The voting was done by secret ballot.
Mrs. Gladys Valentine was re-elected.
Bro. Lemons encouraged each one to pray
for the officers -
    Requirements of church members as
sent out by Springfield was read by
Bro Lemons.
    Church doors were opened for new
members. I joined the Church.
    { Mrs. Alma Biggut }
    { Big June Patterson }

Business meeting held on January 24, 1943, included an election for Brother Paul McKeel as Pastor.

January 24 - 1943 -
A finance committee was appointed
by Bro Lemons for the purpose of raising
money to buy chairs for the church.
The committee consisted of the following:

Rev. J. J. Lemons (Pastor)
E. H. Pinner.
C. D. Demery.
V. L. Bomar.
Edward Hanks.
Mable Demery
Ila Cole
Gladys Valentine.

Business meeting Oct. 17 1943
Meeting called to order by Mr. C. D. Demery
Everyone was called to the altar
for a season of prayer.
Ballots were passed by Bro. Demery
Bro Paul McKeel was put before
the members - They voted a yes
or no ticket.
votes were as following

yes - 15   The vote was so
no - 8   near ⅔ that the
Blank - 1   deacons³ called it
an election - Thus Rev. Paul
McKeel became pastor -

Monthly expenses in 1943 included 60 cents for coal oil and
$1.35 for electricity.

30

		Expense for 1943		3 5 3	
monthly	day	Light bill	Jan. 10	1.	67
1	31	Janitor bill for Jan. paid jan.31.		6	00
2	1	Insurance on parsonage paid Feb.1.		7	84
2	7	Borrowed money Mr. Higgins	" 7	3	.84
2	14	Coal Oil	" 14		.60
2	22	Bolts for seats	" 22		.40
Bal.		Paid on living room suite for parsonage		29.	80
2	15	Bal. on Coal (canning factory)		6	.25
2	10	Electricity bill		1	.35
1	11	Ledger			.65
				58.	40

March					
mar. 8		Electricity	$1	.35	
mar. 23		ton Coal (Shelton motor co	9.	00	
mar. 27		Janitor bill Feb. + mar.	$12.	00	
mar. 28		5 gal. Coal oil		.60	
			$22.	95	

April.				2 2	
april 10		Electricity	1.	35	
april		For shingles to patch roof	2.	38	
april 25		Janitor bill for april	6.	00	
may 1.		Lumber for Bookcase	4.	53	
may 6		Gasoline, brooms etc.	4.	80	
may 10		Electricity	1.	35	
may 16		Lumber for book case	2.	55	

Silver Anniversary (1950-1959)

The church turned 25 in 1954, but there were no records found that indicated any sort of celebration. The records found for the 1950s included cash ledgers, business meeting notes, and Sunday School attendance books carefully preserved by Peggy (Pinner) Cox. Some items of interest included the Sunday offering, which ranged from a total of $81.15 on December 17, 1950, to $175.57 on January 16, 1955. On May 25, 1953, $149.63 was paid to build a concrete footing for the "Sunday School unit." An "organ fund" included donations from church families, mostly $5 - $10 each. The phone bill was $3.65 in November of 1952 and the light bill was $11.32 in January 1955. Brother Earl Pritchard was paid an offering of $70 each week.

Some of the more interesting board meeting notes in the 1950s included a decision made on February 18, 1952, to "eliminate all business meetings from Sunday morning when it interferes with morning worship." On May 14, 1952, church members voted for Pastor J. W. Gladney to serve an indefinite term rather than the one year terms that had been voted on previously. According to the minutes, "The vote was 100% for Bro. Gladney, and all the people said 'praise the Lord.'" On February 11, 1953, another discussion about the pastor's tenure resulted in a decision to elect the pastor for two-year terms, and "Bro. E.F. Pritchard was elected."

Janice (Valentine) Greathouse reflected on her time growing up in the church, "Our church has always been known for its music. We started a radio program called Echoes of Calvary, and they did the service live as soon as church was over at 12:30. I remember on Sunday nights we didn't have air conditioning, and they would raise the windows up on both sides of the church. I can remember going out, and there would be cars parked on the road here, and all they did was stop to hear the music. They loved to come and hear the music from our church. We have always been blessed with a strong musical program" (J. Greathouse, personal interview, May 2, 2013).

Dorothy (Valentine) Williams, also remembers the importance of music in the church. "He (Pastor Pritchard) came to the fields where we were chopping cotton... and he told my older sister, Polly and I, that he wanted us to sing in the choir, and later on we had a radio program that aired on WKBL, in Covington. Cathy Pritchard and Doris (Cole) McKenzie and I were the Echoes of Calvary Trio....and later on Jan (Greathouse) and J.T. (Forbess) and Martha (Pinner) Watkins (and Thurston Starnes) were the Calvary Echoes Quartet. Carolyn Combs later replaced Martha Watkins after Martha moved out of state. Patsy (Valentine) Skinner played piano and also sang with the quartet (D. Williams, personal interview, May 7, 2013). The radio program continued for approximately 20 years until it was discontinued in the 1970s.

Healing is a large part of the church history. At the height of the polio epidemic, members of the church were also affected. Peggy (Pinner) Cox recalls her healing touch. In 1948 or 1949, Peggy awoke one morning to find her legs would not work. Dr. Nichols came to the home, and told her mother the bad news: He suspected polio. Arrangements were made for Peggy to have tests. Her mother stayed home with Peggy's brother and sister and prayed, while Emery and Bessie Pinner took Peggy to the hospital. Peggy recalls hearing her grandparents praying all the way to Memphis. The spinal tap was done, and when the results came from the lab, the doctors gave the good news, "No she does not have polio." The family members knew without a doubt that God had healed Peggy on the way to the hospital (Cox personal interview, December 11, 2013).

The polio scare renewed a lot of people's faith in healing. "They didn't know how it started, where it was coming from, or if it was a virus or some sort of bacteria. They just didn't know. That summer in Memphis they shut down public areas like the movie theatres and the swimming pools. It was almost like a ghost town of sorts because this epidemic was there, and they didn't know how it was being transferred from one person to the other" (Cox, Greathouse, & Williams personal interview, December 11, 2013).

Dorothy Williams described how God healed her sister, Janice (Valentine) Greathouse, from polio in July 1950. "Mother and my older sisters had walked the floor all night with Jan crying. A few days before mother had taken our sisters, Pat and Jan, to the Munford clinic, Pat remembered mother called on the doctor to come to our house. The doctor stood her down to let her walk, and when he did, her legs folded up on her, and he said, 'Mrs. Valentine, I hate to tell you this, but I believe your baby has polio.' They didn't know where it came from and everybody was afraid of it" (Williams personal interview, December 11, 2013).

Bill Williams and his wife, Doris, (now deceased) prayed as they knelt beside their bed, "We're going to pray for baby Jan. Bill was given the assurance that she was going to be ok. That baby is going to be okay. God's going to heal her" (Williams personal interview, December 11, 2013).

Others in the church also prayed for healing. Six men left the church on a Sunday night and went to the hospital in Memphis. They were not allowed in the hospital, so they stood at the curb and prayed for her.

This healing had a great impact on many people associated with the church, including many who were children at the time. "Aunt Loree's two daughters, Doris and Joyce, and I and one of our cousins from Memphis were over at Grandma's house. Joyce said we're going to take this pillow, and this is going to be Janice. In other words, this is our point of contact. We're going to pray, and we just had the assurance that God was going to heal her. God did heal her, so that was our family testimony of God's healing and his protection over her all these years" (Williams, personal interview, May 7, 2013; Greathouse & Williams personal interview, December 11, 2013).

"Just look at the impact this has made on so many people. For one thing, we have Jan and Peggy, and the Lord has multi-talented them. But another thing, we have that foundation. If God can do it then, he can do it now. Just like the Children of Israel going through the Red Sea. If He can send the cloud by day and the fire by night, and see them through the wilderness, nothing is impossible" (Williams personal interview, December 11, 2013).

Historical events from the 1950s (source: U.S. Census Bureau)

- Presidents of the United States: Harry S. Truman and Dwight D. Eisenhower.
- U.S. Population: 151,325,798.
- RCA broadcasts the first color television program on June 25, 1951.
- Sam Phillips opens the "Sun Records" record label in Memphis, TN, March 27, 1952.
- Francis Crick and James Watson discover the spiral structure of DNA on February 28, 1953, and report the findings in *Nature* on April 25, 1953.
- Memphis DJ Dewey Phillips introduced radio listeners to Elvis Presley on July 8, 1953, when he played "That's All Right" on his "Red, Hot, and Blue show."
- Ernest Hemingway's *The Old Man and the Sea* receives a 1953 Pulitzer Prize. In 1954, the author is awarded the Nobel Prize in Literature.
- The *USS Nautilus*, the first nuclear submarine, launches on January 21, 1954.
- On December 1, 1955, Rosa Parks refuses to vacate her seat aboard a Montgomery, AL, bus.
- Fred Gipson publishes the novel, *Old Yeller* in 1956 and receives a Newbury Honor in 1957.
- CBS debuts *Leave It to Beaver* on October 4, 1957.
- Brazil wins its first Federation Internationale de Football Association (FIFA) World Cup, beating Sweden 5-2, on June 29, 1958.
- Alaska and Hawaii become the 49th and 50th states, respectively, in 1959.
- Rod Serling's *Twilight Zone* begins airing October 2, 1959.

Cost of living (source: U.S. Bureau of the Census, *Historical Statistics of the United States, Colonial Times to 1970, Bicentennial Edition, Part 2.*, Bureau of Labor Statistics, 2011)

Flour (5 pounds)	49 cents
Bread (1 pound)	14 cents
Round Steak (1 pound)	94 cents
Bacon (1 pound)	64 cents
Butter (1 pound)	73 cents
Eggs (1 dozen)	60 cents
Milk (1/2 gallon)	41 cents
Oranges (1 dozen)	50 cents
Potatoes (10 pounds)	46 cents
Coffee (1 pound)	79 cents
Sugar (5 pounds)	49 cents

"A Full House." Congregation photo taken in 1953.
Photo courtesy of Bill and Dorothy (Valentine) Williams.

Lanelle (Bomar) Timbs' Sunday School Class (circa 1950).
Photo courtesy of Ruth Rogers Grissom.

Left to Right Back Row:
Peggy Layton Hathcock
Wesley Tierce
_____Conley
Jimmy Hamblin
Melvin Elam
Bryson Jackson
Donald Campbell
Lanelle Timbs
Ruth Rogers Grissom

Seated Left to Right:
Freda Wolfe
Shelby Wilson
Joyce Ann Cole Stapleton
Ann Belk Morgan
Shelby Davidson Myles
Dorothy Valentine Williams
Helen Starnes Kirkland
Ruby Valentine Byrd

Pictured in this family photo (circa 1950) are Martha (Pinner) Watkins, Peggy (Pinner) Cox, Nancy Byrd, and Bessie Pinner. Photo courtesy of Peggy (Pinner) Cox.

Pictured in this family photo taken on October 19, 1952 are Gracie
(Rogers) Myles, Linda (Myles) Mashburn, Ruth Rogers (Grissom),
Brenda (Faye) Myles, and Alfred William Myles, Sr.
Photo courtesy of Linda (Myles) Mashburn.

This photo labeled, "Transportation Day," includes Pastor J. W. Gladney and Sunday School Superintendent Spencer Cole. Photo courtesy of Loree (Millican) Cole.

TRANSPORTATION DAY
PASTOR — Rev. J.W. GLAdNey
S.S. SUPT. S.Cole 1950's

Pictured are Pastor Earl Pritchard, Vacation Bible School Superintendent Doris Williams, and Sunday School Superintendent Spencer Cole.
Photo courtesy of Loree (Millican) Cole.

5- PASTOR- REV. EARL PRITCHARd
V. BS. SUPT. DORiS WiLLiAMS
S.S. SUPT, S, COLE

The Gladneys served the church from 1951-1953.

Brother Gladney, Gordon Gardner, Sister Gladney (circa 1950).
Photo courtesy of Bill and Dorothy (Valentine) Williams.

Pastor Earl Pritchard and family,
who served the church from 1953-1963.
Photo courtesy of Bill and Dorothy (Valentine) Williams.

Bob Bryson and Ken Forman. Evangelists for Crosstown Revival
(circa 1950)

Attendance and finance records from 1956-1960. Attendance in 1956 averaged 240 Sunday morning and 200 Sunday evening. The church building value was $50,000 in 1959, and the parsonage was valued at $9,000. Debt ranged from $1,000 in 1956 to $3,000 in 1959.

Date	No. of Members	Attendance Sun. A.M.	Sun. P.M.	Church value	Parsonage value	Debt
'56	96	240	200	40,000	5,000	1,000
'57	98	175	175-190	40,000	7,000	1,600
'58	98	195	200	50,000	"	1,200
'59	90	185	200	"	9,000	3,000
9/60	89/163	185	190	75,000	7,000	800.

Church Turns Forty (1960-1969)

Church members celebrated the 40th anniversary of First Assembly of God in 1969. Part of the celebration included a directory complete with a history of the church and photos of leaders, staff, and families. There were 85 families pictured in the directory.

Reverend C. Milford Hicks accepted the pastorate from Reverend E. R. Driver in July 1966. During Brother Driver's tenure, church members installed central air conditioning for the first time. Church members did not want to go into debt, so they asked for donations. Enough was collected to pay for the upgrade. Central air is something many people take for granted today, but it was a big deal during this time period according to those who were members of the church at the time. The parsonage was also built during Brother Driver's time at the church.

According to the welcome letter from Pastor Hicks, "Christian workers from Munford Assembly of God Church have had a part in establishing churches at Covington, Detroit, Brownsville, Simonton, Wrights, Warren, Millington, Bolton, Midway, and Mt. Lebanon. Munford Assembly of God Church is very actively engaged in fulfilling the great Commission of our Lord Jesus Christ. The Church presently helps support fifteen missionaries working in fifteen countries. Various ministries such as schools, orphanages, Teen Challenge, Inner City Evangelism, and Revival Time, are also in our missionary budget. Among our Tennessee Assemblies of God churches, the Munford Church ranks second in various ministries giving."

One common theme I heard while interviewing members of the church was helping those in need. One powerful testimony was shared by Shirley Brown whose family received financial help from members of the church during a time of need in 1964. Her testimony is included at the end of this chapter.

Historical events from the 1960s (source: U.S. Census Bureau)

- Presidents of the United States: John F. Kennedy and Lyndon B. Johnson.
- Population: 179,323,175.
- On July 15, 1960, Senator John F. Kennedy accepts the Democratic nomination for president at Memorial Colliseum, Los Angeles, CA.
- After 13 years, NBC cancels *Howdy Doody*. The last episode airs September 24, 1960.
- Harper Lee's 1961 book *To Kill A Mockingbird* is a bestseller.
- On October 1, 1962, James H. Meredith becomes the first black student to attend the University of Mississippi.
- Betty Friedan's 1963 book *The Feminine Mystique* critiques the myth that a woman's identity is linked to childrearing and the accomplishments of their husbands.
- The Beatles make their U.S. debut on *The Ed Sullivan Show*, on February 9, 1964.
- The 9th Marine Expeditionary Brigade arrive in Vietnam on March 8, 1965.
- Apollo astronauts Virgil Grissom, Edward White, and Roger Chaffee die during a simulated launch exercise on January 27, 1967.
- Western movie hero John Wayne wins the 1969 Best Actor Oscar for his role in the movie *True Grit* beating now legendary actors Richard Burton, Peter O'Toole, Dustin Hoffman, and Jon Voight.
- The August 1969 Woodstock Music and Art Fair draws more than 450,000 people to Bethel, NY.

Cost of living (source: U.S. Bureau of the Census, *Historical Statistics of the United States, Colonial Times to 1970, Bicentennial Edition, Part 2.*, Bureau of Labor Statistics, 2011)

Flour (5 pounds)	55 cents
Bread (1 pound)	20 cents
Round Steak (1 pound)	$1.05
Bacon (1 pound)	66 cents
Butter (1 pound)	75 cents
Eggs (1 dozen)	57 cents
Milk (1/2 gallon)	52 cents
Oranges (1 dozen)	75 cents
Potatoes (10 pounds)	72 cents
Coffee (1 pound)	75 cents
Sugar (5 pounds)	58 cents

FIRST ASSEMBLY OF GOD

Beaver Road   *Munford, Tennessee*

40th Anniversary

1929 - 1969

HISTORY OF OUR CHURCH

The First Assembly of God Church, Munford, Tennessee dates its origin from a tent revival conducted at Glenn Springs in the summer of 1928 by evangelists Raymond Wiseman and William A. Bridges. The meeting drew tremendous crowds with many souls being saved and filled with the Holy Spirit. Miraculous healings also caused many to believe.

Later the tent meeting was moved to Crosstown, Tennessee. Out of these meetings was laid the foundation for the present church. At first there was no permanent sanctuary and services were conducted from house to house.

The first church was set in order in the home of Mr. and Mrs. Emery Pinner. The Rev. A. T. Hickman, Tennessee District Superintendent of the Assemblies of God, presided over the meeting. There were 31 charter members of whom there are 21 still living. Seven charter members are a part of the present congregation.

On December 24, 1929 the foundation for the first church was laid. The congregation has suffered the loss of two churches by fire. The present sanctuary is the third building to house the church. During these times of misfortune the Munford Presbyterians graciously provided the use of their church.

Christian workers from the Munford Assembly of God Church have had a part in establishing churches at Covington, Detroit, Brownsville, Simonton , Wrights, Warren, Millington, Bolton, Midway, and Mt. Lebanon.

Ministers who have gone out from the church are Mervin Gross, Dixie Purser, Robert Delancey, Bessie Pinner, and Earnest Carter. Presently, one of our young men, James Mayer is studying for the ministry at Central Bible College, Springfield, Missouri.

Munford Assembly of God Church is very actively engaged in fulfilling the great Commission of our Lord Jesus Christ. The Church presently helps support fifteen missionaries working in fifteen countries Various ministeries such as schools, orphanages, Teen Challenge, Inner City Evangelism, and Revival Time, are also in our missionary budget. Among our Tennessee Assemblies of God churches, the Munford Church ranks second in various ministries giving.

The Rev. C. Milford Hicks is the present pastor. Bro. Hicks accepted the pastorate July 1966 succeeding the Rev. E. R. Driver.

Youth Camp in 1960.
Pictured are Doris (Delashmit) Glass, Demmy Pritchard,
and Peggy (Pinner) Cox.
Photo Courtesy of Janice (Valentine) Greathouse.

Youth Camp at Shelby Forest in 1962.
Pictured are Linda (Poston) Patrick, Paula (Moore) Hoover, Janice
(Valentine) Greathouse, and Patsy (Valentine) Skinner.
Photo Courtesy of Janice (Valentine) Greathouse.

Missionette Group (1967).
Pictured are Josie Pickard, Gladys Valentine, Dotty (Pinner) Rice,
Liz Williamson, Linda Layton, Martha (Pinner) Watkins, Linda
Layton, Patsy (Valentine) Skinner, Janice (Valentine) Greathouse.

Missionette Group Making Flowers for Mother's Day in 1967.
Liz Williamson, Peggy (Pinner) Cox, Patsy (Valentine) Skinner,
Dorothy (Valentine) Williams, Martha (Pinner) Watkins.

1969 Church Directory Photos

Sunday Morning Services

Womens Missionary Council

Missionettes and Sponsors

Church Nursery Attendants

1969 Church Directory Photos

Church Board and Pastor
1969

Sunday School teachers and officers

Church Choir

IN MEMORIAM

C. D. Demery

Mrs. Hazel Valentine

Mrs. Doris Williams

Photo of Pastor C.M. Hicks taken in June 1967.
Pastor Hicks served from 1966 until his death in 1972.
Photo courtesy of Peggy (Pinner) Cox.

A resolution passed on January 30, 1962, appointing a board of directors in addition to the deacon and trustee board.

RESOLUTION

JANUARY 30, 1962

WHEREAS MEN ARE INDESPENSABLE TO THE WORK OF GOD, AND GOD HIMSELF RECONIZES THIS TO BE SO, AND WHEREAS WE FEEL THAT THE MEN OF THIS CHURCH SHOULD BE FILLING A MORE ACTIVE PLACE IN ITS ACTIVITIES.
BE IT RESOLVED:

A) THAT THERE BE A BOARD OF DIRRECTORS IN ADITION TO THE BECON AND TRUSTEE BOARD NOW EXISTING.
    THOSE CONSTITUTING THIS BOARD WILL BE THE PASTOR, AND DECONS, THE TRUSTEE'S TOGATHER WITH THREE OTHER MEN NOMINATED AND ELECTED AT THIS MEETING.

B) THIS BOARD SHOULD FUNTION ONLY IN MATTERS OF BUSINESS :IN THE PURCHASING OF PROPERTIES, OR THE SALE OF SAME,IN EXPANDING OR GENERAL REPAIRS OF PROPERTIES OWNED BY THE CHURCH, AND ANY OTHER MATTERS OF BUSINESS OF A SECULAR NATURE.

C) THE DECON BOARD SHALL CONTINUE TO FUNTION IN THE CAPICITY IN WICH THEY DO NOW FUNTION, ACTING WITH THE PASTOR IN ALL MATTERS OF A SPRITUAL NATURE, AND IN INFORCING THE DECIPLEN OF THE CHURCH.

SUBMITTED BY THE PASTOR AND DECON BOARD, AND WE MOVE ITS ADOPTION.

E.F.PRITCHARD....................PASTOR.

created adopted.

Board meeting held September 14, 1964, included the approval of two pecan trees on the lawn of the parsonage. The board also agreed to pay $1.25 per hour for a part time secretary for Pastor Driver. "It was suggested that Mrs. Driver fill this position."

Board Meeting this Sept 14 1964

Meeting Called to Order by Rev Driver
Reading Proverbs 12 Chapter.
Prayer by all

No 1. talk of Putting Trees on The Lawn of New Parsonage 2 Pecans in back 2 maple in front. Bro Driver to contact Mr Boys about this.

No 2 Nominations for Sunday School Teachers be made by Church members only also all Teachers be members of this Assembly.

No. 3. Nominations for Sunday School Supt. be made by the Teaching Staff and later screened by the board.

No 4. The board agreed to let Bro Driver have a part time secetary and pay 1.25 per hour for this service. It was Suggested Mrs Driver fill this position.

No 5 we agree to pay for the radio time out of the regular Church fund since we have no funds in the Broadcast account.

No 6 Bro Paul Pickard is to get the light poles in Bro Jess Cale Pasture which was placed there several years ago for a recreation field by the Church.

Dismissed with prayer By Bro Driver

Board meeting held January 18, 1965, included approval of a public address system for approximately $250.

Board Meeting Jan 18 1965

Meeting Called to Order By Rev Driver
Scripture Proverbs 16 Chapter.
Prayer By Bro Paul Valentine
Reading of minits + Finance Report By W.J. Cale
No 1) Talked of Rev + Mrs Driver attending
Ministers Retreat at Gatlinburg, Tenn;
it was agreed to send them and Put up the
Ten Dollar Deposit.
No 2) next the P.a. System was Talked
over Rev Driver had Checked on Price
and it would Be about $250.00 the board
agreed to let him get it.
No 3) The Date for annual Business
Meeting was set to be Feb 3. after this
there was a discussion on the
Constitution and By-Laws for the
Munford Church that Bro Driver
had drawn up.
        Meeting adjourn
        Prayer By W.J. Cale
Present
Rev Driver   Bro Paul Pickard
Bro Spencer Cale   Bro Dewey Frizzell
Bro John Moore   Bro. C.D. Demeny
Bro Jess Cale   Bro Paul Valentine

Board meeting held January 27, 1966, included nominations for deacons, trustees, and directors.

Board Meeting this Jan. 27, 1966

Meeting Called to order By Bro Driver
Scripture reading Proverbs 28 Chapter
Prayer was said by all.

This meeting was mostly to Sieve out
nomination That was made by the Church
Members for new board members to be
elected at the annual Church business
meeting

	Trustee	Directors
For Deacon	Paul Pickard	Gordon Dorn
Spencer Cale	Jess Cale	Bob Bolen
Paul Pickard	Spencer Cale	Billy Belk
Bill Williams	Bill Williams	Bob Hanks
Bobby Bolen	Leon Campbell	Jess Cale
	Gordon Garner	John Moore
	Bob Hanks	Bill Williams
	Paul Valentine	Paul Valentine

Sec + Treas:
Jess Cale, Bob Bolen
Bill Williams

Elton Valentine
Willie Hamblin, Virgil Bonner

Brother Driver urged everyone to attend the Dist
Council meeting at First Assembly Feb 8-10.
We will Elect Delegates to attend Council at the
annual Business meeting. and Because of
our annual Business meeting first Week in Feb
and Council meeting second week in Feb our next
Board meet will be in Mar. Monday Mar 14, adjourned
Prayer By Driver

Board meeting held December 10, 1967, included an increase in the expense offering for Pastor Hicks due to "much traveling back and forth to visit sick in the hospital." The additional $20 each week increased the total weekly pay to $127.

Dec. 10, 1967.

The Board had a meeting this was to consider an expense offering for the Pastor as he has so much traveling back & forth to visit sick in hospital.

It was agreed By the board to give Rev Hicks 20 dollars more each week which will make his total weekly Pay 127 dollars

They also agreed to give him an extra $100.00 dollars for Christmas

Rev. W. E. Lindsey is to speak for Rev Hicks on Dec 24 in morning Service. a short service will be held from 5 till 6 P.M. on Xmas Eve Bro Lindsey is to recieve $20.00 for his service.

On Wed night Dec 27, Bro Paul Pickard will have Charge.

meeting adjourned.

W. J. Cale Sec & Treas

Deacons   Directors

Bro John Moore   Bro Paul Valentine
Bro Paul Pickard   Bro E. H. Pinner
Bro C. D. Demery

Attendance and finance records from 1961-1973. Attendance in 1961 averaged 195 Sunday morning and 230 Sunday evening. In 1961, the church building's value was $75,000, the parsonage was valued at $8,000, and there was a $600 debt.

Date	Members	Adherents	Attendance		Yearly Report	Church Value	Parsonage Value	Debt
			Sun. A.M.	Sun. P.M.				
9/18/61	103	none	195	230	149	75,000.	8000.	600.
9/10/62	105		165	160	135			
8/1/63	89	240	150	100	120	45,000	6,000	
8/10/64	91	250	150	100	121	45,000	18,000	
2/2'66	94	260	125	100	110	50,000	18,000	
1/20/67	93	200	140	135	117	50,000	25,000	
1/10/68	93	200	140	135	117	50,000	25,000	
1/13/69	92	200	140	200	118	"	"	
1/19/70	80	232	140	90	110	60,000	25,000	
1/15/71	95	200	170	140	133	130,000	25,000	
1/27/72	96	200	170	140	133	130,000	25,000	
4/9/73	95	260	180	150	138	100,000	25,000	
1/7/74	100	265	200	175	150	100,000	25,000	

Remarks

Testimony by Shirley Brown
(S. Brown, personal interview, December 1, 2013).

I had four girls. My baby girl was born in 1964. One of the older girls contracted mumps at school. Even though I tried to keep them separated so the whole family wouldn't get sick, it didn't work. Then, I had to go to the hospital for emergency surgery. While I was hospitalized, my husband took care of everything. The bad part was he had never had the mumps. He got the mumps, and since he was taking care of our baby and the whole household, he was unable to take care of himself properly and had a bad setback.

He was unable to work for about six weeks, and therefore there was no income. So here we are: I have a sick husband, three girls now back in school, a newborn, and I am recovering from emergency surgery. The bills are coming in, but there is no money to pay them. I did not know what we were going to do. Being a Christian and taught to trust in God, I just laid the bills out (house note, electric, telephone, etc.) and knelt down in front of the couch in the living room. I said, "You know, Lord, these bill have to be paid. I have no way of doing it. I'm just asking you to take care of it."

This was on a Wednesday night, prayer meeting night. A few minutes later somebody knocked on my front door. It was B. Jack Demery, who was a deacon in our church. He said, "Shirley, we had a little business meeting after the prayer meeting tonight, and we thought you might need a little help. So, we decided that we would take up a love offering for you. He gave me every penny that we needed, every penny. And you know that was a miracle. God hears us no matter what.

Golden Anniversary (1970-1979)

Church members celebrated their 50th Anniversary in 1979 with three former pastors (W.A. Bridges, G. Preslar, W.E. Lindsey) serving as guest speakers. According to a photo caption from the October 10th *Covington Leader*, planning for the 50th Anniversary parade was led by Tom Reynolds, Rev. Charles Hurst, Gaylon Combs, Steven Hurst, and Dwayne Cole. The theme of the youth group float, according to Dwayne Cole, was "Building Faith for 50 years" (D. Cole, personal interview, October 3, 2013). This was one of 10 floats along with other entries in the parade.

Reverend C. M. Hicks had a desire to build a new sanctuary, but it was not in God's plan. In October 1972, Pastor Hicks passed away. Many longtime members still remember receiving this sad news and the current stained glass behind the baptismal was dedicated in Pastor Hicks' memory. According to Dorothy Williams, who was serving as secretary-treasurer at the time, the pattern for the stained glass came from a Christmas card.

The current sanctuary building was completed in September 1974, while Reverend Wayne Bradley was serving as pastor. According to Dorothy (Valentine) Williams, the church borrowed money for the expansion and paid the note off early. "It was wonderful how the Lord blessed us to get this building paid off in full before five years was up. Because I kept thinking, you know, you pray over the people (who) give their tithe and offering and everything else was clicking along. We didn't stop missions or anything. The Lord blessed us" (D. Williams, personal interview, May 7, 2013).

The first baby dedicated in the new sanctuary was Bill and Janice (Valentine) Greathouse's daughter, Ashley. Ashley serves as the discipleship pastor at Englewood Church in Independence, Missouri.

The Valentine women have a long history of service in the church, and that history was recognized in 1970 when Gladys Valentine was awarded the Tennessee Women's Ministry President of the Year.

In 1975, J. Samuel Rasnake wrote *Stones by the River: A History of the Tennessee District of the Assemblies of God.* Munford First Assembly plays a large role in the 11th chapter of the book, where Rasnake describes the history of the church as well as the current leaders. Rasnake also noted that, "There were 262 enrolled in Sunday school, and the church gave more than $400 per month to twenty-eight missionaries in 1972. The present property is valued at more than $250,000" (Rasnake, 1975).

For a number of years in the late 1970s-1980s the church had a large bus ministry made possible by volunteers like Allen and Barbara Hanks and Charles, Lea Hambick, and JoAnn Hambick. Charles Hambick continues to serve the church today working selflessly behind the scenes preparing communion and setting up chairs and tables for various events at the church throughout the week. Charles provides a great example of humble faithful service.

The bus ministry originally started in the 1950s, according to Dorothy Williams. Bill (Williams) was instrumental in getting a bus. "We had a church bus, and it was a city street bus….wasn't a school bus. Bill made connections for the church to purchase that bus, and ….we got a lot of people into Sunday School and in church. Elton Valentine was the bus drive" (D. Williams, personal interview, May 7, 2013).

According to Dwayne Cole, "The old bus (in the 1980s) was painted a bright blue and it was called the hallelujah bus" (D. Cole, personal interview, October 3, 2013.

Many of the photos for this chapter were provided by Faye Ellis. She was very active in the church and earned the Missionette Sponsor of the Year in 1977.

Korean War Veteran and Purple Heart Recipient, Robert "Bob" Ellis, shared his memories of the church and how his decision for Christ changed his life, "The Easter Sunday I got saved (April 4, 1972), I never will forget it. I really felt like a newborn" (R. Ellis, personal interview, May 8, 2013).

Bob is one of the many military veterans who currently attend the church, and there is a great deal of patriotic support for the men and women who wear the cloth of our nation defending our freedom. Faye Ellis recalled the prayers for her grandson who served multiple combat tours in Iraq and Afghanistan, "He has a scar where the bullet grazed his eyebrow. I mean, that is God heavily protecting him" (F. Ellis, personal interview, May 8, 2013).

Throughout the decade there was a great deal of growth in attendance and church expansions. The most important growth continued to be prayer, worship, and support to missions.

Historical events from the 1970s (source: U.S. Census Bureau)

- Presidents of the United States: Richard Nixon, Gerald Ford, and Jimmy Carter.
- Population: 203,302,031.
- The Ohio National Guard opens fire on protesters at Kent State University, killing four and wounding nine on May 4, 1970.
- The Organization of Arab Petroleum Exporting Countries announces an embargo on oil exports to the United States on October 15, 1973.
- President Richard Nixon resigns from office on August 8, 1974.
- The last Americans (10 U.S. Marines) depart Vietnam on April 30, 1975.
- Michael Shaara's *The Killer Angels*, a novel about the Battle of Gettysburg, wins the Pulitzer Prize for Fiction in 1975.
- NASA's Viking 1 lands on Mars on July 20, 1976.
- The miniseries *Roots* airs from January 23 to January 30, 1977. The series would earn 36 Emmy nominations and win 9.

Cost of living (source: U.S. Bureau of the Census, *Historical Statistics of the United States, Colonial Times to 1970, Bicentennial Edition, Part 2.*, Bureau of Labor Statistics, 2011)

Flour (5 pounds)	59 cents
Bread (1 pound)	24 cents
Round Steak (1 pound)	$1.30
Bacon (1 pound)	95 cents
Butter (1 pound)	87 cents
Eggs (1 dozen)	61 cents
Milk (1/2 gallon)	66 cents
Oranges (1 dozen)	86 cents
Potatoes (10 pounds)	90 cents
Coffee (1 pound)	91 cents
Sugar (5 pounds)	65 cents

Board meeting held on September 17, 1970, to discuss borrowing money to pay for new annex. A motion passed to borrow $30,000 on a six-year loan at 7.5% interest.

Board Meeting Sept 17-70

The Church Board of Officials Called This meeting to discuss borrowing Money from Munford union Bank to pay for new Annex.

Motion was made by Paul Pickard and Seconded by Bill Williams to borrow Thirty Thousand on six year loan at 7½ Per cent.

They also agreed to put in American Standard Air Condition.

The Board Also agreed Not to build Foundation for new Auditorium at Present, this was Put in form of Motion Bill Greathouse Made Motion Seconded By Bill Williams

It was also agreed by Board to go ahead and Brick Front where the Blocks Are,

J. J. Forbess and Bill Greathouse Are to Check on some Signs for our Church and also make some Pictures for the Church of those Present for the meeting

Deacons Paul Pickard Bill Williams J. J. Forbess

Trustee's Paul Valentine John moore Bill Greathouse,

Sec + Treas W. J. Cole

Ground Breaking Ceremonies, July 6, 1970. Rev C. M. Hicks, pastor of the Assembly of God Church of Munford, breaks ground for a new $40,000 addition to the church Sunday afternoon. Church deacons taking part in the ceremonies are (left to right) Paul Valentine, John Moore, Jess Cole, Paul Pickard, Rev. Hicks and Bill Williams. The addition will house the pastor's study, recreation hall, kitchen and ladies' lounge.

Ground Breaking Ceremonies

Rev. C. M. Hicks, pastor of the Assembly of God Church of Munford, breaks ground for a new $40,000 addition to the church Sunday afternoon. Church deacons taking part in the ceremonies are, l to r, Paul Valentine, John Moore, Jess Cole, Paul Pickard, Rev. Hicks and Bill Williams. The addition will house the pastor's study, recreation hall, kitchen and ladies' lounge. July-6- 1970

Services for Rev. Hicks On Sunday

Rev. Clessie Milford Hicks, minister of Munford Assembly of God Church for the past seven years, died on Oct. 27 in Methodist Hospital in Memphis where he had been a patient for the past three weeks after suffering a heart attack. He was 63.

Rev. Hicks was born on Aug. 11, 1909, in Grenville County, Mo. He had been a minister for 42 years serving churches in Tennessee, Georgia and Illinois.

Services were on Sunday at 3 p.m. in Munford Assembly of God Church with Rev. Earl Blythe officiating. Interment was in Helen Crigger Cemetery with Munford Funeral Home in charge.

Rev. Hicks is survived by his widow, Mrs. Evelyn Beatrice Robertson Hicks; two sons, Rev. Robert Hicks of Marianna, Ar., and Rev. David Hicks of Johnson City; two daughters, Mrs. Carol Jean Crouch of West Memphis, Ar., and Mrs. Mary Ruth McDaniel of Orlando, Fl.; two brothers, Harold Hicks of Fontana, Ca., and Willard Hicks of Granite City, Il., and two sisters, Mrs. Dorothy Utley of Granite City and Mrs. Florence Hanover of Belleville, Il.

Groundbreaking ceremony held on December 9, 1973, for the new sanctuary. Included in this photo were Thurston Starnes, J. T. Forbess, Mayor Robert Wooten, John Moore, Reverend Wayne Bradley, Bill Williams, Bill Greathouse, and Paul Pickard. (*The Covington Leader*, December 13, 1973)

Groundbreaking

Official board members of the Munford Assembly of God Church witnessing the groundbreaking on Sunday of the new sanctuary are, l to r, Thurston Willie Starnes, J. T. Forbess, Mayor Robert Wooten, John Moore, Rev. Wayne Bradley, Bill Williams, Bill Greathouse and Paul Pickard.

"The Munford Assembly of God Church is planning a parade on Saturday to kick-off a week of festivities celebrating their 50th anniversary. Planning the event are seated (left to right) Tom Reynolds, adult departmental superintendent; Rev. Charles Hurst, pastor; Gaylon Combs, junior and senior high superintendent. Standing is Steven Hurst, Sunday school superintendent, and Dwayne Cole, assistant Sunday school superintendent. The parade is scheduled to begin at 11 a.m. and is expected to have around 10 floats, along with other entries. All day services on the Sunday will be led by Rev. Ray Hundley of Indianapolis, IN. The 2 p.m. service will honor three of the church's first pastors. They are William Bridges, W. E. Lindsey and George Preslar. The Sunday service also kicks off a week of revival at the church." *The Covington Leader*, October 10, 1979.

OCT 1 0 1979

FURNISHED BY YOUR
FRIENDS AT THE

FSB First State Bank
COVINGTON, TENN.

Published in The Covington Leader

Plans Parade

The Munford Assembly of God Church is planning a parade on Saturday to kick-off a week of festivities celebrating their 50th anniversary. Planning the event are seated (l to r) Tom Reynolds, adult departmental superintendent; Rev. Charles Hurst, pastor, and Gaylon Combs, junior and senior high superintendent. Standing is Steve Hurst (l), Sunday School superintendent and Dwayne Cole, assistant Sunday school superintendent. The parade is scheduled to begin at 11 a.m. and is expected to have around 10 floats, along with other entries. All day services on Sunday will be led by Rev. Ray Hundley of Indianapolis, In. The 2 p.m. service will honor three of the church's first pastors. They are W. M. Bridges, W. L. Lindsey and George Preslar. The Sunday service also kicks off a week of revival at the church.

Pictorial Directory

50th Anniversary
First Assembly of God
P.O. Box 806
Munford, Tennessee
Phone 837-8105

The Opportunity to Minister. . .1979

W.M.C.'s

Christ Ambassadors Officers

Missionettes

Prims

Daisys

Mrs. Velma Stimpson - Nursery

Royal Rangers

Children Church Workers

Church Bus Workers

"The Opportunity to Praise With Music"

Steve Hurst Minister of Music

Patsy Bomar - Organist

Sanctuary Choir

All God's Children

"Little Children" Rejoice

The Opportunity to Worship

Pastor Rev. Charles Hurst

Associate Pastor Rev. Keithel Boothe

Board of Deacons

Sunday School Superintendents

50th Anniversary guest speakers included former pastors
William Bridges, George Preslar and W. E. Lindsey.

Photos from the First Assembly of God Church
50th Anniversary Parade in Munford, TN on October 13, 1979.

"The Munford Assembly of God Church had popsicle day for the children's church department on Sunday. A giant popsicle was frozen and placed on the church lawn. Following the worship service each child was given a popsicle."
(*The Covington Leader*, October 4, 1978)

THE MUNFORD Assembly of God Church had popsicle day for the children's church department on Sunday. A giant popsicle was frozen and placed on the church lawn. Following the worship service each child was given a popsicle.

Miss Mile of Dimes in a 1978 photo. Pictured are Sandra Booth, Penny Jo Pitt, Faye Ellis and Betty Whitehust. Photo courtesy of Faye (Cole) Ellis.

MISS MILE-OF-DIMES, Sandra Booth (front row, l), and Little Miss Mile-Of-Dimes, Penny Jo Pitt (front row, r), raised the most money from their mission group, the Missionettes of the First Assembly of God Church in Munford, which will be used for missionary support. Their leaders (back row, l to r), Faye Ellis and Betty Whitehurst, sponsored a banquet for the mission group members, escorts and parents on Friday evening in the church fellowship hall. Guest speaker was Melba Cole of Memphis.

Miss Mile of Dimes in 1978. Photo courtesy of Faye (Cole) Ellis.

Miss Penny Queen. Photo courtesy of Faye (Cole) Ellis.

Ladies Sunday School Class and Missionette Group

Ladies Sunday School Class
1970's
Willie Clay Adkinson - Teacher

Missionette Group
1970
Gladys Valentine and Josie Pickard

Missioneettes photo courtesy of Faye (Cole) Ellis.

Fall Convention at Memphis First Assembly of God in
September 1975. Photo courtesy of Faye (Cole) Ellis.

Attendance records for 1974-1983. Sunday morning attendance ranged from 200 in 1974 to 250 in 1979. Church value increased from $100,000 in 1974 to $250,000 in 1979.

	Members	Adherents	Attendance Sun. A.M.	Sun. P.M.	Yearly Report	Church Value	Parsonage Value	Debt
1/7/74	100	265	200	175	150	100,000	25,000	
2/31/74	110	233	200	200	155	200,000	25,000	
/25/76	103	228	225	225	164	---	35,000	
2/14/77	108	300	200	100	154	200,000	25,000	
1/17/78	--	300	200	100	225	200,000	35,000	
2/9/79	120		250	100	185	250,000	incl	none
2/11/80	120	300	275	125	198	195,000	55,000	none
3/9/81	115	300	230	125	183	----	60,000	none
2/4/82	125	300	225	125	175		---	none
/10/83	100	300	250	150	175	800,000	50,000	none

Remarks:

Stones by the River: A History of the Tennessee District of the Assemblies of God by J. Samuel Rasnake (1975). Information about Munford First Assembly of God Church can be found in Chapter 11 (pages 132-133).

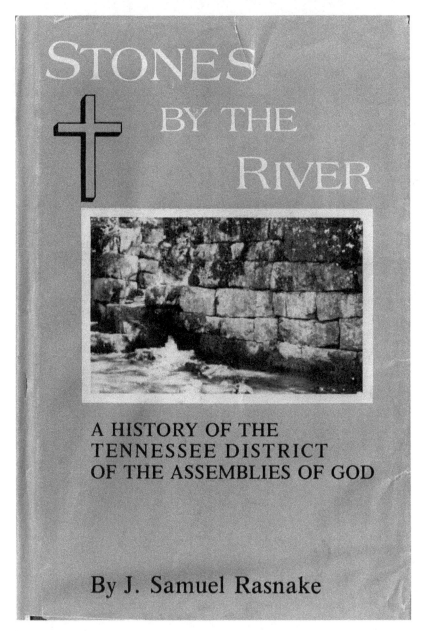

Pastor and Mrs. C.M. Hicks

Pastor
+
Mrs. C. M. Hicks

Pastor 1966 - 1972
Deceased
10 - 27 - 1972

The baptismal is dedicated in memory of Reverend C. M. Hicks.

60 Years Young and Still Growing! (1980-89)

The decade began with a major expansion known as the Lindsey Center Multi-Purpose Building. Reverend W. E. Lindsey was a former pastor and long-time member of the church. Today, it serves as a gymnasium for the community where youth play basketball and participate in other activities. The building also serves the community once a month as part of River of Life's ministry to help feed the hungry in Tipton County. Church volunteers, in coordination with the Mid-South Food Bank, join residents from the local community to serve those less fortunate. On Sunday mornings the building is used for Children's Church, and on Wednesday evenings boys and girls are mentored to evangelize, equip, and empower the next generation of Christ-like servant leaders.

According to longtime board member and church leader, Bill Greathouse, "The gym was really a miracle. People were just so concerned because we were borrowing, I think it was like $80,000 or something, and they said, 'How are we ever going to pay this money back?' and we actually paid it off in seven years. We have always been good about paying off debt. People have risen to the occasion" (B. Greathouse, personal communication, April 30, 2013).

Church members celebrated the 60th anniversary of the church with a special service and a program that noted, "Through the years two education units have been added, a larger auditorium, a parsonage, and a gymnasium. Many churches throughout West Tennessee have been established and are a strong witness today because of Munford First Assembly. There have also been a number of people who have been called into ministry. For approximately 20 years the church had a weekly radio broadcast on WKBL in Covington, TN. The church is known for its Music Department. During the Easter and Christmas season people throughout the area came to worship with us" (River of Life 60th Anniversary Program).

Sheila Cole reflected on the music ministry during this time. "One thing I remember about the early 80s was the choir. We had a huge choir. Steve Hurst was the music minister, and they were always working on an Easter or Christmas cantata. It was a huge draw for the community because people would come for miles to hear the music" (S. Cole, personal interview, October 3, 2013).

According to Dwayne and Sheila Cole a major revival was held at the church in 1988 with Ralph Duncan. "I remember the altars being filled with people…(who) acted like they didn't want to go home" (D. and S. Cole, personal interview, October 3, 2013).

Janice Greathouse also remembered the revival, "We had a six-week revival with Ralph Duncan, and we had church every night except Saturday. We had it two weeks, and then he came back and had another four weeks, and the church was full every night. We would start at 7 o'clock, and it would be 11 or 12 usually at night before church service was over" (J. Greathouse, personal intereview, May 2, 2013).

"The 80s were a grand time," according to Bill Greathouse. "Brother and Sister Hurst, their only son, Steve, is a tremendous music person. The choir and everything stepped up to a new level. We pushed 300 (attendees) during those times, and they did a lot of special Christmas (programs) and Easter music" (B. Greathouse, personal interview, April 30, 2013).

Another example of healing occurred during Reverend Hurst's tenure. According to Dorothy (Valentine) Williams, Sister Hurst was diagnosed with cancer, and members of the church prayed in her behalf. God intervened to heal her. Today she is living in Nashville, TN, doing well, and serving the Lord (D. Williams, personal interview, December 11, 2013).

Historical events from the 1980s (source: U.S. Census Bureau)

- Presidents of the United States: Ronald Reagan and George H.W. Bush
- Population: 226,542,199
- On April 12, 1980, the United States Olympic Committee voted to boycott the Summer Olympics in Moscow in response to the Soviet invasion of Afghanistan.
- Mark David Chapman murders John Lennon outside the Dakota Hotel in New York City, NY, the evening of December 8, 1980.
- Prince Charles and Lady Diana marry at Westminister Abbey on July 29, 1981.
- The musical *Cats* debuts on Broadway, October 8, 1982. It would hold the record for most performances (7,484) until surpassed by *The Phantom of the Opera* in January 2006.
- Apple Computer® launches its Macintosh computer in 1984.
- The Space Shuttle Challenger explodes 74 seconds after liftoff on January 28, 1986.
- Chris Van Allsburg's *The Polar Express* wins the 1986 Caldecott Award.
- The stock market loses 22.6 percent of its value on "Black Monday," October 19, 1987.
- Sylvester Stallone stars in 1988's *Rambo III* following the success with *Rambo: First Blood* (1982) and *Rambo: First Blood Part II* (1985).

Cost of living (source: The People History)

Bacon (1 pound)	$1.69
Bread (1 pound)	50 cents
Flour (5 pounds)	99 cents
Ground Beef (1 pound)	$1.39
Margarine (1 pound)	50 cents
Milk (1 Gallon)	$1.59
Oranges (1 dozen)	$1.39

Ground Breaking Photos for the W.E. Lindsey Center,
October 25, 1981. Photo courtesy of Peggy (Pinner) Cox.

Lindsey Center Multi-Purpose Building Ground Breaking Program
October 25, 1981

GROUND BREAKING
LINDSEY CENTER - MULTI-PURPOSE BUILDING
OCTOBER 25, 1981

I. CALL TO WORSHIP
We are assembled at this place to open the ground which shall receive the foundation of the Lindsey Center, which, by the grace of God, we have determined to build. Since we have been taught that all important undertakings should always begin by seeking divine guidance, let us by scripture and by prayer invoke God's leadership upon us.

II. SCRIPTURE
I Cor. 3:9-17

III. SINGING OF DOXOLOGY

IV. CONSECRATION (Minister and people shall say together).
We the people of this congregation do now, in the presence of God and in reverence to His Holy name, dedicate ourselves to the end:
That the house designated for this place shall be a monument to His grace;
That whatever is within our power to further its construction, both by gifts and by service, we will do;
That it shall exalt the Lord Jesus Christ, both in its service to God and to man.

V. DECLARATION (The Minister shall say)
To the glory of God and in the presence of this congregation, I now request that ground be broken for the new Lindsey Center Multi-Purpose Building in Munford, Tennessee. Upon you as members of this congregation rests the responsibility and privilege to cause the Lindsy Center to rise here which shall be devoted to honor almighty God our Father, and His blessed Son and our Savior, Jesus Christ.

VI. BREAKING OF GROUND

VII. RESPONSIVE PRAYER
Minister and people: Almighty and everlasting God, in communion with the saints in all ages, and remembering the heritage that has been given to us, we offer Thee our praise and thanksgiving.
People: O Lord, hear our prayer.
Minister: Enable us, by Thy grace, to dedicate ourselves this day to the great task which Thou dost lay upon our hearts and consciences.
People: In all that we do, be Thou, O Lord, our strength and help.
Minister: Reveal to us the beauty of Thy perfect law, the joy of our living Lord, so that with glad hearts we may move forward in paths of high devotion and great achievement.
People: Be Thou, O Lord, our Guide and help forevermore. Amen.

VIII. PRAYER OF DEDICATION

IX. DOXOLOGY

Lindsey Center Pledge Card

Pastor and Mrs. W.E. Lindsey

Reverand and Mrs. W.E. Lindsey

Application for Membership circa 1980

APPLICATION FOR MEMBERSHIP

Having personally experienced the New Birth (John 3:5-8), through faith in the atoning blood of the Lord Jesus Christ; and having considered favorably the doctrines and practices of the Assemblies of God, and being in complete agreement with them; and desiring to be associated with those of like precious faith in Christian fellowship, I hereby apply for church membership.

I agree to be governed by the rules of the church, to attend the means of grace regularly as I have opportunity, and to support its ministries with my tithes and offerings as God shall prosper me.

It is my earnest prayer that God shall keep me true to Him, but if for any reason I shall depart from the faith, or cease to live a godly life, or change my doctrinal beliefs, I shall consider it just, to be automatically released from membership in the church.

Date .... Signature ....

To Be Completed by Pastor

Manner Received ....
Date ....

Name of Church ....

Pastor's Signature ....

(Over)

REQUIREMENTS FOR MEMBERSHIP

Spiritual Experience. Each candidate for membership shall be expected to give a clear testimony of having been born of the Spirit of God (John 3:5-8), and of having received the Holy Spirit or to be earnestly seeking to be baptized in the Holy Spirit (Acts 2:2-4).

Water Baptism. It is expected that each candidate will follow the scriptural command to be baptized in water by immersion in the Name of the Father and of the Son and of the Holy Spirit (Matthew 28:19).

Word of God. The candidate must have a sincere belief in the inspiration of the Holy Scriptures as the Word of God and the final authority in all matters of faith and conduct.

Separation. Association with the church should indicate cessation of worldly practices such as the use of alcoholic beverages, tobacco, narcotics, the practices of gambling, dancing, and attendance at theaters and other places of questionable amusements (2 Corinthians 6:14-17; Romans 6:4).

Return of the Lord. The candidate must have a hope and expectancy of the premillennial return of the Lord Jesus Christ.

Spiritual Growth. The candidate should develop the practice of daily prayer, Bible study, personal witnessing, and faithful attendance at worship and observance of the sacraments.

(Over)

Form No. 07-5268   Gospel Publishing House, Springfield, Mo. 65802   PRINTED IN U.S.A.

Choir photos from 1981-1983 courtesy of Jennifer Poston.

Church Directory Photos from 1985

Official Board
1985

Women's Ministries
1985

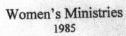

Sunday School
1985

Sunday School
1985

Sunday School 1985

Sunday School
1985

Board of Deacons and Sanctuary Choir 1989

Thurston Starnes   **BOARD OF DEACONS**   **Bill Greathouse**
J. T. Forbess   **1989**   **John Wells**
Pastor Windell Splawn   **Spencer Cole**

SANCTUARY CHOIR Directed By John Wells

Women's Ministries, Sunday School Teachers, Officers and Bus Ministry 1989

WOMEN'S MINISTRIES

1989

SUNDAY SCHOOL TEACHERS, OFFICERS AND BUS MINISTRY

Children's Church, Missionettes, Prims and Rainbows 1989

CHILDREN'S CHURCH
Director of Children's Ministries
Jo-an Hambick

1989

MISSIONETTES, PRIMS, AND RAINBOWS AND SPONSORS

Ministry to Boys and Light Brigade 1989

MINISTRY TO BOYS
1989

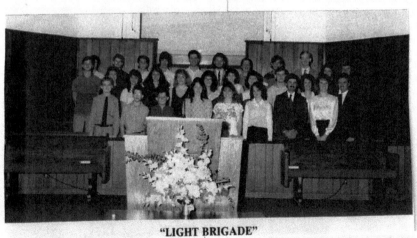

"LIGHT BRIGADE"

Billboard Sign on Highway 51 (circa 1980)

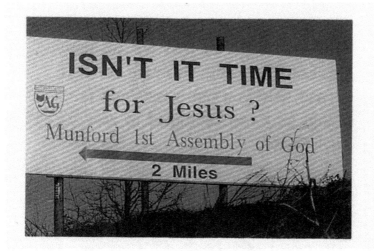

The Valentine family was chosen as the 1981 "Family of the Year" by the Tennessee District Women's Ministries Department.

FAMILY of the YEAR
The PAUL VALENTINE FAMILY

"We have been blessed by our Christian heritage," are the words of Mr. & Mrs. Paul Valentine. Their family has been chosen to be honored as the 1981 "Family of the Year" by the Tennessee District Women's Ministries Department. Coming from Baptist and Methodist backgrounds respectively, the families of both Brother and Sister Valentine became members of the Assemblies of God when they were filled with the Holy Spirit. In fact, Sister Valentine's parents were charter members of the Assembly of God in Munford, when it was set in order in February, 1929. Today, she and her husband, along with various children and grandchildren, still serve in various capacities in the ministry of that church. Sister Valentine is known for her commitment to the work of Women's Ministries.

The Valentines were married in 1935. Brother Valentine was a farmer. In fact, he still farms, along with his brother Elton. In younger days, he served as deacon for the church, devoting many hours of manual labor to its various building projects. They have always been faithful in attendance and in giving.

One by one, their four daughters were born and dedicated to the Lord. First was Bonnie Pauline (Polly); then Dorothy Marie, followed by Patsy Gale and Janice Corrine. A very great trial of their faith occurred when their baby Janice was stricken with polio at the age of two. Though doctors offered little hope for the child, in response to the prayers of hundreds of people, God miraculously touched her and not only spared her life, but kept her from becoming crippled.

Today, all four girls are happily married and rearing children of their own. In 1957, Polly married Dr. Robert H. Donald, and ENT specialist. He was in the Navy, stationed in Millington. Soon he was sent to California, where daughters Judy and Debbie were born; then, to Japan, where baby Cathy joined the family. Upon his release from the Navy, Bob and Polly moved to Tuscaloosa, Alabama. While there, they were blessed with a little boy, Robert David. He was followed by Michael Paul.

Now, Judy is a senior at U. T. in Knoxville. She
plans to work in the field of Human Services. Debbie
works as a veterinarian assistant. Cathy is preparing
to be a pediatrician at the Walters State College in
Morristown. Bobby is a freshman at the Tennessee
School for the Blind, and Mike attends junior high in
Morristown, planning to become a doctor.

In February, 1967, Dorothy became the bride of Blake
(Bill) Williams. He was a widower with a teenage son
Jimmy. Jimmy now resides in Memphis and is employed by
DuPont as an operator. Dorothy and Bill have one son,
Blake. He attends Munford Ellis Junior High, and is a
member of the Drum Corp. He is a Trailblazer in Royal
Rangers and enjoys baseball. Dorothy is active in her
church, singing in the choir and as soloist for the
Munford Funeral Home. She has taught Sunday School,
served as Sunday School Secretary, and currently teaches
Nursery II class. She is the church secretary and
treasurer and is employed by the City of Munford as City
Recorder.

Dorothy's husband Bill is a native of South Carolina.
He has served as a church board member, taught Sunday
School and served as secretary for the Men's Bible
class. He is employed by Gateway Motors in Millington.

In 1964, Patsy Valentine graduated from high school
where she had been a dedicated band member developing
a great love for music. She was a member of the National Honor Society during her junior and senior
years. She currently serves as church organist and
teaches Sunday School. She was married to Robert Nor-
man Bomar of Munford in September, 1967. He is employed by International Harvester and Patsy serves as
an executive secretary for Sears.

Janice graduated in 1966. She, too, enjoyed band
and received the John Phillip Sousa Band Award. She
now teaches Sunday School and is an active choir member.
She married William (Bill) Greathouse of West Virginia,
in November, 1968. For ten years, they have worked as

sponsors of the Munford Assembly C. A. Department. Bill has served a board member, Sunday School teacher for the Young Married Couples Class, been active in Royal Rangers and ministered with the MAPS program in Puerto Rico. He is currently employed in Jackson, where he is Purchasing Manager for Tabuchi Electric Co. Janice works part time as a medical secretary for the Methodist North Internal Medicine Group.

She and Bill have two children: Ashley, born in August, 1974 (an active Daisy and Brownie Scout); and Marty, born in May, 1978. At 2½, Marty is all boy, loving ball, combines, tractors, puppies and—Jesus! His is a strong faith that has been filtered through Mother, Daddy, aunts, uncles, grandparents, and great-grandparents. In the words of Brother and Sister Valentine, "WHAT A HERITAGE!"

May God richly "BLESS THIS HOUSE". It is truly a remarkable "Family of the Year" to which we give honor.

"As for me and my house we will serve the Lord" (Joshua 24:15).

Music, Missions, and Children's Ministries Continue to Reach the Community (1990-99)

On September 11, 1994, church members celebrated their "65th Anniversary and Homecoming." The church continued to grow, especially in the areas of music and children's ministries. Hundreds of families from the local community visited the church in 1998 to witness a special drama called, "Heaven's Gates and Hell's Flames." Churches continue to share this drama with their local communities around the world, and River of Life shared the drama again in 2012.

Reverend Gene Burgess led the church as pastor from 1991-1999. Pastor Burgess was a pharmacist, which helped him gain entry into many countries as a missionary. He was able to heal physically and spiritually. "Brother Burgess was a missionary when he came to us. That was a good time for the church because we have always been mission's minded" (B. Greathouse, personal interview, April 30, 2013).

In 1999, a record of baptisms from 1940 was assembled. While this record is not all-inclusive (e.g. there are no recorded baptisms from 1941-1959) it is remarkable that someone invested the time to assemble this information. It's just one more example of the important role that others who have gone before us played in the creation of this book. Without their dedication, devotion to record-keeping, and preservation this historical account of our church would not be possible.

Children's ministry was active through the Royal Rangers and Missionettes (now called Mpact Girls Clubs). Sheila Cole remembers her time teaching Rainbows with her sister, Cindy. "We taught for several years. Some of the kids who are graduating (high school) now were our Rainbows. This past (high school) graduation season Pastor told me that one of the students who applied for the ministerial scholarship wrote in her scholarship essay that she was saved in our Rainbow class...I love my Rainbows" (S. Cole, personal interview, October 3, 2013).

Historical events from the 1990s (source: U.S. Census Bureau)

- Presidents of the United States: George H.W. Bush and Bill Clinton
- Population: 248,709,873
- On August 2, 1990, the Iraqi army invaded Kuwait. When negotiations failed, the United States-led coalition of military forces attacked the Iraqi Army in January 1991 and officially liberated Kuwait on February 25, 1991.
- A 51-day standoff in Waco, TX, begins when agents from the Bureau of Alcohol, Tobacco, and Firearms attempt to arrest Branch Davidian leader David Koresh on February 28, 1993.
- Matthew Broderick is awarded the 1995 Best Actor Tony Award for his role in the musical "How to Succeed in Business Without Really Trying."
- Celine Dion's *Falling Into You* wins the 1996 Album of the Year Grammy.
- Diana Princess of Wales dies in a Paris car accident, August 31, 1997.
- At age 77, John Glenn becomes the oldest astronaut in space on October 29, 1998.
- The Dow Jones Industrial Average closes above 10,000 for the first time on March 29, 1999.

Cost of living (source: The People History)

Bacon (1 pound)	$1.24
Bananas (1 pound)	48 cents
Eggs (dozen)	$1.05
Ground Beef (1 pound)	$1.09
Margarine (1 pound)	49 cents
Milk (1 Gallon)	$1.90

65th Anniversary & Homecoming Program, September 11, 1994

FIRST ASSEMBLY OF GOD

Gene Burgess — Pastor
Mark Kirkpatrick — Youth Pastor
Melody Kirkpatrick — Music Minister
Jo-an Hambick — Children's Minister
Carol Sweetman — Secretary/Outreach

****

65TH ANNIVERSARY & HOMECOMING
September 11, 1994

Sunday
9:00 AM Prayer in Sanctuary
9:30 AM Sunday School
10:45 AM Praise and Worship
- Rev. Gene Jackson
- NO Children's Church
NOON Buffet (Lindsey Center)
2:00 PM Special Homecoming Program
** NO evening service

Monday
7:00 PM Marriage Enrichment Seminar
7:00 PM Prayer Meeting at Mary Mayers

Tuesday
10:00 AM Ladies Bible Study at Parsonage

Wednesday
6:30 PM Moms In Touch Prayer Meeting
7:00 PM Youth Pastor's Prayer Partners
7:30 PM Royal Rangers
7:30 PM Missionettes
7:30 PM Youth Meeting
7:30 PM Young Adult Bible Study (Parsonage)
7:30 PM Young Couples Bible Study (Parsonage)
7:30 PM Adult Bible Study

Saturday
9:00 AM Nursing Home Ministry in Covington

A NURSERY IS PROVIDED FOR ALL SERVICES
****

This morning there will be NO Children's Church. We ask that all children ages 5 & up to stay with their parents during the service. Today is a special day for the whole family to enjoy together.

RENOVATIONS HAVE CONTINUED - The latest project we have undertaken is vinyl siding for all the exterior wood surfaces. In the upcoming months our goals are to re-carpet and re-decorate the sanctuary, add another ladies room and increase our nursery capacity by one third.

MARRIAGE ENRICHMENT SEMINAR - Join us tomorrow night at 7:00 PM at the Munford Recreation Center across from City Hall. See advertisement on back table for more details.

MINISTER'S RETREAT - Let's keep Pastor & Mrs. Burgess in prayer as they attend the Minister's Retreat in Gatlinburg, TN this week. They will return Friday afternoon. Pastor Mark will be available in case of emergency.

FOREVER YOUNG...is planning a trip to Eureka Springs, AR Oct. 25-28. Cost is $125-140 for lodging and entry into events such as: Passion Play and a concert. If there is considerable interest we will go. Please sign-up on the bulletin board.

NEW MEMBERS CLASS - A special orientation class called "The Blessing of Belonging" will begin next Sunday morning at 9:30 am in the choir room. This class is designed for those who would like to know more about our church and are considering church membership. Taught by Pastor Burgess. For more information contact the church office.

C O N G R A T U L A T I O N S - On Saturday September 3, Mark & Melody Kirkpatrick became proud parents of Andrew Mark Kirkpatrick who weighed 7 lbs 6 oz and was 19 3/4 inches long. We pray God's blessings on the family and this precious new life.

M I S S I O N E T T E B A K E S A L E

Next Sunday after the morning service we encourage you to support our girls.

BAKE SALE

65TH ANNIVERSARY & HOMECOMING
FIRST ASSEMBLY OF GOD
MUNFORD, TN

SEPTEMBER 11, 1994
2:00 PM - 3:30 PM

Choruses	Pastor Mark Kirkpatrick
Opening & Welcome	Pastor Gene Burgess
Steve Hurst & Sanctuary Choir	
Special Recognition	
Welcome - Recognition of Guests	
Offering	Pastor Gene Burgess
Offeratory	Steve Hurst
Choir	Directed by: Steve Hurst
"We Remember When"	Gladys Valentine
	Loree Cole
	Adele Layton
	Mary Sue Poston
Special Music	DeLancey & Jean Gladney
Former Pastors	Rev. Charles Hurst
& Staff Members	Rev. Ernest Driver
Share	Rev. Keithel Boothe
	Rev. Bob Greathouse
Benediction	

Special Gifts at door for all adults and children.

** The flowers in the sanctuary have been placed
   in loving memory of Rev. & Mrs. Wreed Gladney
   by their children.

Ushers and Greeters (circa 1990)

Munford Assembly of God Ushers
Winford Pinner, Don Campbell,
Mike Murphy, Bill Greathouse
1990's

Greeters - 1990's
Don Campbell
Tom & Gladys Reynolds
Greeting Jack Carroll

Greeters - 1990's
Lilly Icenhour & Gladys Reynolds
Greeting Dorothy Williams

Photos courtesy of Peggy Cox

Men's Fellowship (circa 1990)

Men's Fellowship
1990's

Men's Fellowship
1990's

Photos courtesy of Peggy Cox

Women's Fellowship 1992

WM Ladies at WM Retreat
1990's

Photo Courtesy of
Janice Valentine Greathouse

Louise Delashmit
Gladys Valentine
Mary Sue Poston
1992

Hazel Kuykendall
Gladys Valentine
Elizabeth Hamblin   1992
Lottie Downing

Sunday School (circa 1990)

Sunday School Class
for 5 year olds
Teacher: Shelly Gough

Sunday School Class
for Middle School
Teacher: Mike Starnes

Sunday School Class
for High School
Teacher: Bill Greathouse

Sunday School (circa 1990)

Sunday School Class
for Ages 2 and 3 year olds
Teachers: Dorothy Williams,
Dotty Rice, Judy Brooks

Sunday School Class
for Ages 4 year olds
Teacher: Patricia Murphy

Sunday School Class
for Second Grade
Teacher: Peggy Cox

Sunday School Class (circa 1999)

Sunday School Class
Second Grade – 1999
Clayton, Stephen, Ashton
Peggy Cox

Sunday School Class
2 & 3 year olds
1990's
Teachers: Dorothy Williams
Judy Brooks & Cindy Mathis

Ladies Sunday School and Young Adults Fellowship (circa 1990)

Ladies Sunday School Class
1990's

Fellowship
1990's

Young Adults Fellowship
1990's

CHRISTMAS COMES TO LONE STAR GULCH

CAST

Marty Greathouse	Mr. Johnson
Jonathan Mayer	Mr. Mayor
Amy Dick	Mrs. Mayor
Greg Cox	Sheriff Duke
Howard Brooks	Parson
Amanda McCraw	Schoolmarm
Stephanie DeHart	Becky Jones
Paul Greathouse	Tom Pickens
Matthew Cooper	Matthew
Sonya Blizzard	Townsperson
Tabitha Hawkins	Townsperson
Jennifer Maddox	Townsperson

CHOIR

Allen Blizzard	Marcy Mathis
Austin Blizzard	Melanie Murphy
Angie Burns	Bart Numera
Kathryn Cole	Teaha Numera
Lindsey Combs	Novie Price
Regina Forbess	April Rice
Christy Hopper	Nicole VanDouser
	Jamie Vinson

Photo Courtesy of Peggy (Pinner) Cox

Christmas Comes to Lone Star Gulch centers around a small, turn-of-the-century, western town celebrating Christmas. Everyone is happy except Storekeeper Johnson, who doesn't know the real meaning of Christmas. Through a small child and the townsfolk, however, Mr. Johnson finally realizes that Jesus is the reason for Christmas and that Jesus can make a difference in your life.

We hope that you will allow Jesus to make a difference in your life and thank you for allowing us to share this message with you!

Director:	Jo-an Hambick
Staging:	Michael Murphy
Prompter:	Patricia Murphy
Costumes:	Janice Greathouse
Props:	Cindy Mathis
Sound:	John Earl Wells, Dwayne Cole
Lights:	Bill Greathouse
Helpers:	Larena DeHart, Judy Brooks, Betty Vinson, Lia Hambick, Sheila Cole, Dotty Rice, Barbie Cooper, Herbert Cox

Youth Group 1991-1992

Youth Group
1991
Going to Convention

Youth Group
1992
Going to Convention

Youth Group
Photos Courtesy of Judy Brooks.

Congregation group photo taken circa 1994

Missionettes (circa 1990)

Missionette Group
1990's

Missionette Group Leaders
1990's
JoAnn Hambick, Ruth Vath, Lorena DeHart,
Martha Watkins, Jackie Roe, Dotty Rice, Jo Ann Daniels

Missionettes 1998

Missionette Group
1990's

Missionette Group
1998
Honor Stars
Lindsey Combs, Carolyn Combs
Janice Greathouse

Royal Rangers.
Photo Courtesy of Judy Brooks.

Vacation Bible School
Peace Patrol: Solving Spiritual Mysteries 1994
Photo Courtesy of Peggy (Pinner) Cox

New Carpet 1995
Photo Courtesy of Peggy (Pinner) Cox

Munford Assembly
1995
Preparing for New Carpet
for Sanctuary
April & Dotty Rice
Greg Cox & Scooter Brooks
Bob Ellis & Mark Kirkpatrick

New Carpet 1995
Photo Courtesy of Peggy (Pinner) Cox

Munford Assembly
1995
Preparing for New Carpet
for Sanctuary
April & Dotty Rice
Greg Cox & Scooter Brooks
Bob Ellis & Mark Kirkpatrick

1995 - Munford Assembly
April Rice
Bob Ellis & Mark Kirkpatrick

1995 - Munford Assembly
April Rice, Greg Cox, Mike
New Carpet for Sanctuary

1995 - Munford Assembly
New Carpet for Sanctuary
April, Mike, Dotty

Vacation Bible School
Life Call 911: God to the Rescue 1996
Photo Courtesy of Peggy (Pinner) Cox

Vacation Bible School
Life Call 911: God to the Rescue 1996
Photo Courtesy of Peggy (Pinner) Cox

Children's Christmas Program: Super Duper Christmas 1997
Photo Courtesy of Peggy (Pinner) Cox

Children's Christmas Program
1997
"Super Duper Christmas"

Choir in 1997

CHOIR MINISTRY

Youth and Children's Ministry in 1997

**Youth
and
Children's
Ministries**

Day Care Ministry and Children's Ministry 1997

Day Care Ministry
1997

Children's Ministry
1990's

Youth Group Outreach 1997

Youth Group Outreach
1997

Youth Service
1997

HEAVEN'S GATES

AND

HELL'S FLAMES

A Life Altering Drama. Written by Bruce and Ruth Thum, and Chuck Verness

First Assembly of God Church
220 Beaver Road
Munford, TN 38058
(901) 837-8781

Pastor Gene Burgess

Heaven's Gates/Hell's Flames
1998
Angels
Phyllis Roe, Dotty Rice, Judy Brooks, Jo-an Hambick
Erica Valentine, Sherry Glover, Ann Taylor

Childrens Christmas Program: Hark the Herald Angel 1998

Hillbilly Junction Dinner Theatre 1998

Board of Deacons In 1997: Charles Hambick, Bill Greathouse, J. T. Forbess, Pastor Gene Burgess, Gaylon Combs, Don Campbell.

Fellowship Photos (circa 1990)

Forever Young

Honor Bound Men

Church Fellowship Dinner

Golf Tournament

Testimony of Healing for Jeremy Wells
(courtesy of John Earl Wells)

Our son, Jeremy, was attending the University of Memphis in the fall of 1993, when he began having throat infections frequently. After different treatments from his doctor, he did not get better so more tests were done. The doctor called us in and told us that he now suspected that Jeremy had Hodgkin's lymphoma – cancer in the lymph glands that were now swollen. The doctor referred Jeremy to LeBonheur Hospital where more tests were done, and it was determined that Hodgkin's was probably the problem. The nurse even had me feel for the swollen glands because they had become obvious by that time. A biopsy was scheduled on a Monday to remove lymph glands for testing. This had taken many weeks to get to this point so we had been praying for God's healing to occur. On the Sunday before surgery, Jo Anna and I (along with many others) prayed at the altar for God's intervention. He was the first surgery scheduled the next morning so we left early to get there for the outpatient procedure that would last a little more than an hour. After taking him back and being put to sleep, the doctor came to us in just a few minutes and said that when he checked Jeremy's throat area to see where to begin, there was no sign at all of any lymph gland enlargement. So, he cancelled the procedure and told us to come back if it reoccurred (which it has not, twenty years later). Praise God!

Presentation by Janice (Valentine) Greathouse in February 1995 paying tribute to Elizabeth Hamblin, Gladys Valentine, and Mary Sue Poston for their years of service in Women's Ministry.

Presentation given by Janice Greathouse to the congregation in February 1995.

On this Women's Ministries day, we would like to recognize and pay tribute to three very special ladies, Mrs. Elizabeth Hamblin, Mrs. Gladys Valentine, and Mrs. Mary Sue Poston. After years of faithful service and leadership in our WM program, they are now retiring from their positions as president, vice-president, and secretary-treasurer.

Mrs. Hamblin and Mrs. Poston both began actively working in WM's in 1951, and Mrs. Valentine began in 1934. That would be 161 years of collective service to the WM program. This would involve weekly meetings, how many fund raisers—it would be impossible to say, gathering food for Hillcrest, buying linens for our Tennessee missionaries, visiting shut-ins, praying for needs, sponsoring children financially at Hillcrest, cutting off postage stamps for missions, and the list goes on and on.

We want to thank these ladies for their faithful service today. Mrs. Hamblin has served as president since 1984 and has been the President of the Year for the Covington Section seven of the past fifteen years.

Mrs. Valentine served as president from 1934 until 1984, and vice-president from 1984 until 1995. She was President of the Year for the Tennessee District in 1970, which was the first year this honor was given. Mrs. Valentine was again recognized by the Tennessee District in 1993 for 59 years of faithful service to Women's Ministries.

Mrs. Poston has served as secretary-treasurer for the past 30 years of our local group. Just think of all the bank deposits, checks, quarterly reports, and annual reports for which she has been responsible.

One of the scripture verses we have learned in Missionettes is I Timothy 4:12 which says, *"Be thou an example of the believers, in word, in conversation, in charity, in spirit, in faith, in purity."* I believe we have seen this scripture fulfilled in the lives of these ladies. So, on behalf of our church family, we want to formally thank you for your years of service and present you with a gift, as well as a gift from the Missionette auxillary. Only the Lord will be able to repay you for the burden you have carried for the work of Women's Ministries. After our study this week, I can see many jewels in your crowns at the Judgment Seat of Christ for your efforts.

Tonight, the Missionettes will be sponsoring an afterglow to complete our recognition of these ladies. I hope you will make plans to stay and give these ladies a hug.

A New Name, but the Same Passion for Building Families and Growing Faith (2000-2009)

In January 2005, Munford First Assembly of God Church changed names to River of Life Assembly of God Church. According to those who were involved with the name change, there was a desire to reach out to more families in the community. I have spoken with families who are members of this church today who would not have visited, much less joined, an Assembly of God Church. I represent one of those families.

When the Navy moved us here in 2006, we were looking for a non-denominational church because we had good experiences with non-denominational churches at previous duty stations. We did not know much about the Assemblies of God, but what little we thought we knew would have been enough to discourage us from attending. To be clear, this is not the fault of the Assemblies of God, and certainly not an indictment of the loving people who serve at River of Life Assembly of God Church. This was simple prejudice on my part based on second and third-hand information about what others said about the Assemblies of God. Looking back, I'm grateful that we serve a loving God who forgives us and knows us well enough to lead us where He wants us to serve in spite of our limited knowledge and other faults. I'm also grateful for the name change because without it, we (like many other families) would not be here today.

According to Bill Greathouse, "It (name change) was a real spiritual thing. We were in a board meeting, and we just had been praying about some changes that needed to be made and one of the other board members said, 'God just gave me a name, and I just want to throw it out and see what y'all think.' And it was 'River of Life,' and it seemed, wow, you know. That is what we're all about, and that is what we want to be about" (B. Greathouse, personal interview, April 30, 2013).

Although the name changed, the passion for serving others through missions, music, prayer, healing, and other ministries remained strong. An example of this was on August 1, 2009, when more than 100 Tipton County families visited River of Life Church during a "Day of Hope" in Munford. About 75 volunteers offered free health screenings, financial coaching and prayer. Church members also provided free food and clothing to local families. "This was a great opportunity to share the love of Jesus with our neighbors right here in Tipton county," said senior pastor Greg Temke. "We can talk about how we care for others, but putting that talk into action is what matters most. As the saying goes 'people don't care how much you know until they know how much you care.' "

In addition to outreach ministries, there was also a continued focus on healing, which is no surprise because the church was founded in 1929 after a miraculous healing. Two of the most-detailed accounts of healing were offered by Bob and Faye Ellis, both of whom were kind enough to spend some time talking with me about their testimony and shared their experiences in the documents that accompany this chapter. These testimonies represent countless other examples of how God uses River of Life Assembly of God Church members to testify about His healing powers.

Another testimony of healing occurred with Sheila Cole who was diagnosed with cancer in 2004. She and her husband, Dwayne, went to church the night they first got the diagnosis, and members of the church prayed over them. A guest pastor was preaching that night, and he told Sheila, "The Lord is burning it out of you. You shall live and shall not die" (S. Cole, personal interview, October 3, 2013).

"The first diagnosis indicated that the cancer may have spread to the lymph nodes which would require treatment. When the doctor looked at the results again he said, 'It is a stain. It is not cancerous.' When he said that, the Lord spoke to me and said that a stain is where something has been and is no longer there, and that was my healing. I knew that God had removed it. He had burned it out from me" (S. Cole, personal interview, October 3, 2013).

"The Lord heard our prayer. She's cancer free, cancer free for many years now" (D. Cole, personal interview, October 3, 2013).

In 2009, church members celebrated 80 years of service to the community in a homecoming celebration that drew 185 in Sunday morning services. Loree Cole, who was 10 years old when the church was founded in 1929, shared her memories of the Glen Springs revival that eventually grew into the Munford First Assembly of God Church. As the only surviving eye witness to the birth of our church, Loree Cole's speech was a special treat for those in attendance. She concluded her remarks reminding us that, "We think of the past, but we live in the now, and we look to the future. This is Holy ground."

Loree Cole's son and Munford Mayor, Dwayne Cole, presented the church with Senate Resolution 59 from the 106th General Assembly of the State of Tennessee and a resolution from the City of Munford declaring April 26, 2009, as "River of Life Assembly of God Church day." The Senate Resolution read in part, "River of Life Assembly of God Church is truly one of the great religious institutions and is a catalyst for positive spiritual change in our State and Nation, and the members of this exemplary institution should be appropriately honored for their exceptional service to their fellow Christians and to the good people of their community."

Dwayne Cole also shared what the celebration meant to him and the community. "Today, as we appreciate the past, affirm the present, and anticipate the future, we recognize God has helped us in the past; He is helping us in this hour; He will help us in the future. At River of Life Church we are well positioned to impact this community for Jesus Christ. We are well positioned to impact this community and this region for the kingdom" (D. Cole, public speech, April 26, 2009).

Historical events from the 2000s (source: U.S. Census Bureau)

- Presidents of the United States: George W. Bush and Barack Obama
- Population: 281,421,906
- The "dot.com" technology bubble, spanning from 1995 to 2000, peaks when intraday trading on the NASDAQ exchange reaches 5132.52.
- Hijacked airliners crash into the World Trade Center, the Pentagon, and a field in Shanksville, PA, September 11, 2001.
- On October 23, 2001, Apple Computer unveils the first iPod.
- The Space Shuttle Columbia breaks apart during reentry, killing the seven astronauts onboard, February 1, 2003.
- On December 26, 2004, one of the largest earthquakes ever recorded (approximately 9.3 magnitude) creates a tsunami that devastates South Asia leaving more than 230,000 dead.
- Hurricane Katrina, the costliest hurricane in U.S. history, hits southeast Louisiana, August 29, 2005.
- Senator Barack Obama is elected as the first African American president of the United States on November 4, 2008.
- In January 2009, Nickelodian celebrates the 10th anniversary of the hit children's television program "SpongeBob SquarePants."

Cost of living (source: The People History)

Gasoline	$1.26
New Home	$134,150
New Car	$24,750
Bacon (1 pound)	$2.97
Coffee (1 pound)	$3.44
Eggs (1 dozen)	$.89

River of Life Church Staff

Church Staff Photo taken December 8, 2009

Pictured left to right standing are: Jeremy Payant, Bill Greathouse, Nick Holt, Jack Carroll, Eddie Smith, Greg Temke, and Mike Starnes.
Pictured left to right seated are: Linda Vandergrift, Carey Lynn Starnes, Janice Greathouse, Judy Brooks, Jennifer Poston, Linda Mashburn, Jean Geary.

City of Munford Proclamation Presented on April 26, 2009, to Commemorate the Church's 80th Anniversary

City of Munford, Tennessee
1397 Munford Avenue
Munford, Tennessee 38058
(901)837-0171
Dwayne Cole, Mayor
www.munford.com

**Proclamation Honoring
River of Life Assembly of God Church's
80th Anniversary Celebration
April 26, 2009**

WHEREAS, River of Life Assembly of God Church was originally chartered as First Assembly of God Church in 1929 at the home of E.H. Pinner with 31 members, as a result of the great revival of Glen Springs and the Crosstown Revival; and,

WHEREAS, As a result of the great outpourings of God's Spirit and mighty healings, the church continued to grow in faith and in spirit; and,

WHEREAS, For eighty years, the congregation of River of Life Church has sought to fulfill the Great Commission to "preach the Gospel" by focusing on evangelism, world missions, discipleship, and community ministry; and,

WHEREAS, The church has confirmed its commitment to the Kingdom of God by adopting the slogan, "Building Families, Growing Faith;"

NOW, THERFORE, I , Dwayne Cole, Mayor of the City of Munford, Tennessee, do hereby proclaim April 26, 2009 to be River of Life Assembly of God Church Day and do offer sincere congratulations for the past, present and future ministry of this church to our citizens and the people of this community.

Dwayne Cole
Dwayne Cole, Mayor

Dorothy Williams
Dorothy Williams, City Recorder

State of Tennessee Proclamation Presented on April 26, 2009, to Commemorate the Church's 80ᵗʰ Anniversary

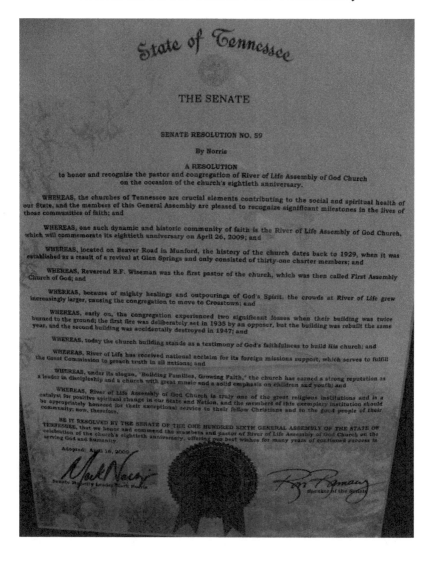

State of Tennessee

THE SENATE

SENATE RESOLUTION NO. 59

By Norris

A RESOLUTION
to honor and recognize the pastor and congregation of River of Life Assembly of God Church
on the occasion of the church's eightieth anniversary.

WHEREAS, the churches of Tennessee are crucial elements contributing to the social and spiritual health of our State, and the members of this General Assembly are pleased to recognize significant milestones in the lives of those communities of faith; and

WHEREAS, one such dynamic and historic community of faith is the River of Life Assembly of God Church, which will commemorate its eightieth anniversary on April 26, 2009; and

WHEREAS, located on Beaver Road in Munford, the history of the church dates back to 1929, when it was established as a result of a revival at Glen Springs and only consisted of thirty-one charter members; and

WHEREAS, Reverend R.F. Wiseman was the first pastor of the church, which was then called First Assembly Church of God; and

WHEREAS, because of mighty healings and outpourings of God's Spirit, the crowds at River of Life grew increasingly larger, causing the congregation to move to Crosstown; and

WHEREAS, early on, the congregation experienced two significant losses when their building was twice burned to the ground; the first fire was deliberately set in 1935 by an opposer, but the building was rebuilt the same year, and the second building was accidentally destroyed in 1947; and

WHEREAS, today the church building stands as a testimony of God's faithfulness to build His church; and

WHEREAS, River of Life has received national acclaim for its foreign missions support, which serves to fulfill the Great Commission to preach truth in all nations; and

WHEREAS, under its slogan, "Building Families, Growing Faith," the church has earned a strong reputation as a leader in discipleship and a church with great music and a solid emphasis on children and youth; and

WHEREAS, River of Life Assembly of God Church is truly one of the great religious institutions and is a catalyst for positive spiritual change in our State and Nation, and the members of this exemplary institution should be appropriately honored for their exceptional service to their fellow Christians and to the good people of their community; now, therefore,

BE IT RESOLVED BY THE SENATE OF THE ONE HUNDRED SIXTH GENERAL ASSEMBLY OF THE STATE OF TENNESSEE, that we honor and commend the members and pastor of River of Life Assembly of God Church on the celebration of the church's eightieth anniversary, offering our best wishes for many years of continued success in serving God and humanity.

Adopted: April 16, 2009

Senate Majority Leader Mark Norris

Speaker of the Senate

Newpaper clipping from *The Leader* April 2009

Mayor Dwayne Cole presents the City of Munford Resolution to Pastor Greg Temke.

Church celebrates 80 years

Day of Hope August 1, 2009

Newpaper clipping from *The Leader* about
The Day of Hope August 1, 2009

River of Life Church hosted a "Day of Hope" in Munford on Aug. 1. Approximately 75 volunteers offered free health screenings, financial budgeting information, and prayer for more than 100 families from Tipton County. Church members also provided free food and clothing for local families as part of the "Nothings too hard for God" campaign this summer.

Newpaper clipping from *The Leader*
about The Day of Hope August 1, 2009

Day of Hope

By ALVIN PLEXICO
Special to The Leader

Munford – More than Tipton County families visited River of Life church Aug. 1 during a "Day of Hope" in Munford.

Approximately 75 volunteers offered free health screenings, financial coaching, and prayer. Church members also provided free food and clothing to local families. River of Life Church members joined volunteers from Baptist Memorial Hospital-Tipton, Tipton County Commission on Aging and National Alliance on Mental Illness.

Children enjoyed inflatable playgrounds, music and games, and one lucky child won an iPod Shuffle for guessing the correct number of Skittles in a jar. Leaders from Royal Rangers and Mpact girls club met with children and parents to discuss the opportunities available through these mentoring ministries.

The "Day of Hope" was the final event in the "Nothings Too Hard for God" campaign River of Life Church members have hosted this summer. Topics shared throughout the series included forgiveness, relationships, and finances.

"This was a great opportunity to share the love of Jesus with our neighbors right here in Tipton county," said River of Life Senior Pastor Greg Temke. "We can talk about how we care for others, but putting that talk into action is what matters most. As the saying goes, people don't care how much you know until they know how much you care."

River of Life offers Sunday school at 9 a.m. followed by worship at 10:15 a.m. Community prayer is Tuesday at 7 p.m. and Wednesday bible study is at 7 p.m. All services include nursery, children and youth programs.

For more information about River of Life Church, visit *www.munfordriveroflife.com* or call 837-8781.

Newspaper clipping from *Tipton Star* about Easter Egg Hunt.
Photo courtesy of Sherry Glover.

Tipton Star

Atoka, Brighton, Drummonds and Munford

The Hunt Must Go On

Saturday's rainy weather canceled or forced several of the community's planned Easter Egg hunts indoors, such as the one held inside Munford First Assembly of God's gymnasium. More than 100 children searched for plastic eggs blindfolded. Sherry Glover, pictured above right, dressed for the hunt in Easter fashion. Three hundred of the 1,800 eggs at the church were donated by the Munford Parks and Recreation Department after its hunt was canceled.

Easter in South Tipton County

Several different Easter activities took place in various locations across South Tipton County this past weekend. In the top picture (l to r), "Special" the clown visits with 15-month-old Addison Cake and her mother, Dawn Cake of Atoka, at First Assembly of God Church in Munford. Pictured to the right is one of the numerous children who enjoyed dying eggs at Munford Presbyterian Church.

Easter activities shared in South Tipton County

Scheduled for Saturday was the City of Munford's annual Easter egg hunt to take place in the city park. But, due to bad weather conditions, the Munford Parks & Recreation Center cancelled this event and donated its approximately 400 eggs with prizes to two local churches.

The recipient churches were Munford Presbyterian Church, located at 25 Tipton Street North and First Assembly of God Church at 220 Beaver Road. Both of these houses of worship conducted inside Easter activities for children and their families on Saturday afternoon.

At Munford Presbyterian Church, visitors were treated to an Easter egg hunt, the making of paper crosses with jelly beans and the dying of eggs. Games such as "musical chairs" and a puppet show were completed. Cookie decorating and face painting were also events

that were enjoyed by the children and a reenactment of the visit to Jesus' tomb was acted out.

Adult volunteers at Munford Presbyterian Church included Hallie Jean Halt, Doris Harkness, Jennifer Turner, Rosemary Arrington, Debbie Scruggs, Liz Bowers, Marsha Deneka, Ann Stewart, Barbara Wenger, Barbara Dorn, Susan Antes, and Elizabeth Garrett.

At the First Assembly of God Church in Munford, Christian music was performed all day as well as "Special" the clown, visited for the afternoon. Visitors were also treated to face painting, a moon walk, an Easter egg hunt and the winning of three larger prizes which were Easter baskets full of prizes.

So, despite the rainy, Easter weather, hundreds of children in the South Tipton County area were still treated to a variety of Easter activities within the community.

Veterans Day Service November 2008. Pictured (left to right) are Alvin Plexico, Lou Parker, Al Lightfoot, Jack Carroll, and Pastor Greg Temke.

Bob Ellis and J. T. Forbess raise the American flag using the flagpole dedicated as part of the Veterans Day Commemoration in November 2008

Veterans gather in front of the flagpole dedicated as part of the
Veterans Day Commemoration in
November 2008

Living Supper Palm Sunday 2009

Century Park Performance.
Photo courtesy of Jennifer Poston.

"Century Park"
A Musical Extravaganza
December 14, 2001

Cast

Keith Adkison	Bob Ellis	Jennifer Poston
Hannah Adkison	Faye Ellis	Bo Quarles
Mark Ballard	Lou Grasser	Judie Quarles
Shari Ballard	Janice Greathouse	Dotty Rice
Sherry Bernard	Charlotte Guinn	Phyllis Roe
Angie Billings	Bill Kelsey	Randy Roe
Judy Brooks	Teri Kelsey	Mitzi Smith
Dwayne Cole	Marilyn Kolbek	Carey Lynn Starnes
Kelly Cole	Michael Laymon	Charles Stoner
Sheila Cole	Marcy Mathis	Linda Vandergrift
Herbert Cox	Lisa McDermott	Martha Watkins
Peggy Cox	Patricia Murphy	JoAnna Wells
Amanda Durham	Buffie Nehms	John Earl Wells
Bonnie D'Andelet	Nancy Pittman	
Dorothy D'Andelet	Carol Poston	

Stage Manager...Cindy Mathis
Wardrobe Coordinator.....................................Jeanine Adkison
Wardrobe Assistants.............................Faye Ellis, Ann Taylor
      Joan McDermott, Sheila Cole, Hannah Adkison, Kelly Cole,
      Melanie Murphy, Sandra Heflin

Christmas Village 2002

Christmas Village
2001
Munford Assembly

Christmas Village
2003
Reindeer Feed Store
Patricia Murphy, Martha Watkins
Ashton and Hannah

Christmas for Children's Church in 2001.
Photos courtesy of Sherry Glover.

God and Country Day 2002

God & Country Day
2002
Gaylon Combs, Perry Pittman, Herbert Cox, Kevin Steel,
Mike Blanchard, Rickey McDermott, Bill Greathouse

God & Country Day
2002
Patricia Murphy, Mike Starnes, Buffie Nelms,
Keith Adkison, Jennifer Poston, Janice Greathouse

Photos courtesy of Peggy Cox

Living Supper 2002

"THE LIVING LORD'S SUPPER"
Palm Sunday Illustrated Sermon
2002
Keith Adkison as "JESUS"

Disciples:

Nathaniel	Dwayne Cole
Andrew	Darrin Rose
James the Less	Mike Nelms
Peter	Perry Pittman
Judas	Troy Davis
John	Michael Laymon
James	Greg Billings
Thomas	Chris Martin
Phillip	Bo Quarles
Matthew	Bill Greathouse
Thaddaeus	Herbert Cox
Simon the Zealot	Gaylon Combs
Woman at the Well	Shari Ballard
Adulteress	Judie Quarles
Pharisees	Carol Poston
	Bruce Taylor

Costume Coordinator	Jeanine Adkison
Sound Engineer	Calvin Kelsey
Lighting	Richard Barnett
	Peggy Cox
	Rickey McDermott
Set Construction	Kevin Wright
	Carey Lynn Starnes

Seamstress':
Bea Wyatt, Faye Ellis, Tammy Wilbanks, Mary Alice Starnes,
Mary Jane Talley, Sheila Cole, Peggy Cox

"Munford Assembly of God Sanctuary Choir"

Keith Adkison	Marilyn Kolbek
Jeanine Adkison	Patricia Murphy
Mark Ballard	Buffie Nelms
Shari Ballard	Nancy Pittman
Greg Billings	Jennifer Poston
Judy Brooks	Dotty Rice
Sheila Cole	Chris Smith
JoAnn Daniele	Carey Lynn Starnes
Bob Ellis	Mike Starnes
Lou Grasser	Charles Stoner
Janice Greathouse	Linda Vandergrift
Rosalind Hunt	Martha Watkins
Bill Kelsey	John Earl Wells
Teri Kelsey	

Nursery photos with Penny Buske and Sherry Glover.

Bob Ellis Testimony

BOB ELLIS' CANCER HEALING

May 2, 2006—Day diagnosis was given by physician. Colonoscopy revealed two tumors in colon, biopsy of each tumor came back malignant. Surgery was scheduled two weeks later on May 17, 2006.

Late Tuesday night, 5-2-06, Jan and Bill stopped by at the request of Bob and Faye. The report was given to Jan and Bill. After talking for a few minutes, we all began to pray over this situation. The first order of business was to cut off the life support of the tumors, speak death to them, and call restoration and life into Bob. Fear was also bound. The following "course of action" was established to bring about Bob's healing.

1. Binding and loosing according to Matthew 16:18-19
   A. Spiritual warfare
   B. Bind tumors and cut off life support (forbid the right to exist)
   C. Curse every malfunction in Bob's body
2. Declarations
   A. Speak God's word over every circumstance
   B. God's Word is life, abundant life, glorious life
3. Rest in the Lord Philippians 4:6-7
   A. Peace, making our needs known unto the Lord with thanksgiving, praise worship in song, prayers, meditation
4. Pray God's Word, listen to healing tapes, quote scriptures in prayer
5. Remind God of His promises
   Early in the AM the Spirit spoke to Faye's spirit, "Whose report are you going to believe? Mine or the doctor's.
6. Call forth manifestation of healing
7. Seal blessings with God's Word by speaking and calling them forth
8. Saturate our environment with praise and worship music
9. Saturate our environment with the Word of God by listening to ministers such as Dr. Creflo Dollar and Rev. Benny Hinn preach and teach on faith and healing.
10. Total peace Philippians 4:6-8
11. Laid ground work, set boundaries, nothing negative. Bill spoke prophetically that Bob was sealed in a golden dome.

May 3, 2006

Make a demand on the enemy.
Remind Jesus of His promise.

This is the prayer prayed over Bob:

Jesus Christ redeemed us from the curse of the law, therefore we forbid any sickness or disease to come upon Bob's body. Every disease, germ, and every virus that touches Bob's body will die instantly in the name of Jesus. Every organ and

Bob Ellis Testimony

tissue of this body functions in the perfection God created it to function and we forbid any malfunction in Bob's body in the name of Jesus (Gal 3:13, Romans 8:11, Gal 1:30, Matt 16:19).

Growths and tumors have no right to inhabit Bob's body. The life of God dissolves growths and tumors and his strength and health are restored (Matt 16:19, John 14:13, Mark 11:23).

Body, we speak the word of faith to you. We demand that every organ perform a perfect work for you are the temple of the Holy Spirit. Therefore, we charge you in the name of the Lord Jesus Christ and by the authority of His Holy Word to be healed and made whole in Jesus name (Proverbs 12:18).

Father, we resist the enemy in every form that he comes against Bob—we command Bob's body to be strong and healthy, and we enforce it with your Word, we reject the curse, and we enforce life in Bob's body (James 4:7).

Monday night prior to surgery on May 17, 2006
Bill and Jan came over for prayer with Bob and Faye for the intended purpose of "taking care of business." This was a group prayer for covering every part of Bob's surgical procedure, environment, doctors, nurses, attendants, medications, etc.

We prayed over the following things:
1. that the doctors and nurses would have guidance and direction from the Holy Spirit
2. no difficulty putting Bob to sleep (answered)
3. all instruments and surgical equipment accounted for
4. no reactions from pain medication
5. no germs, viruses, or diseases on the hands of the doctors, nurses, or attendants
6. the doctor removed one-half of the colon, no cancer cells in the liver, lymph nodes (Bob is cancer free)
7. speedy recovery (doctor said Bob is doing better than ANY patient he has ever had who had this type of surgery)

After prayer Jan stated she saw Bob being held in the arms of four angels, two on each side of him with their arms outstretched holding him. During the surgery he would not be laying upon the metal table, but Bob would be held in the arms of angelic beings watching over him.

On the morning of the surgery, Bob said he envisioned Jesus standing at the head of his stretcher while he was waiting to be taken to the surgery unit. Jesus was holding his head in His hands. Bob went into surgery completely free of fear and was totally relaxed knowing Jesus went with him.

The post-surgical report was that about twelve inches of the colon was removed, along with a fatty sheath of tissue containing the lymph nodes in the stomach area, as well as a suspicious place on the liver. After about two weeks the pathology report brought good news, the tumors in the colon had eaten into the wall of the colon but had not eaten through therefore, the cancer was contained within the removed colon, there were no cancer cells found in the lymph nodes, and the spot removed from the liver was not malignant!

Bob Ellis Testimony

Proverbs 3:25-26, "Don't be afraid of sudden terror because God will keep you strong and firm". Trust in the Lord and His promise. Be open to hear the Word of God's "Whose report are you going to believe? Mine or the doctors." Bob will live and not die.

Philippians 4:6-8, "Do not fret or have anxiety about anything, in every circumstance and in everything by prayer and petition request the needs with thanksgiving. And the peace of God which transcends all understanding shall guard over my heart and mind in Christ Jesus."

Faye Ellis Testimony

Jan 2009

Faye's Testimony

when Annetta ask me to Share my testimony I immediately said yes for God has toonly done a great work in my body —

Listen how I was always in favor + Blessings of the Lord.

As I think back on the year of 2008, it has truly been a challenge for me and my family. As the old saying goes, the year of 2008 came in like a lamb and went out like a lion. I have truly walked through the valley of the shadow of death but I have felt no evil for Jesus was with me. His Word and His Spirit were there to comfort me (Psalms 23:4).

I really had not felt well for a long time. When Jan, Annetta, and I went to Florida, my mind wasn't alert. It was so hard to think and focus, but I faked it. I noticed that I was so tired and I was coughing a lot. I went to the doctor and was treated for Bronchitis. Then on July 25th, Dan Epley and his intercessors came to our church. We visited together with Dan and the team during the day on Saturday and enjoyed being in the presence of the Lord. One of the intercessors said to me, "I see a crown being placed on your head, a waterfall behind you, with purple ribbons unfurling flowing down into the water turning it purple". I pondered what she meant.

Faye Ellis Testimony

By Sunday, I was not able to come to church. Sunday night, Bill & Jan and Lou & Annetta asked if they could come over to celebrate Annetta's birthday and have cake. Their true motive was to come and intercede for me. This is Annetta's account of what she accessed.

After arriving at Faye's house, it became clear that was having a hard time breathing. She was coughing and audibly wheezing. I brought my stethoscope and asked her if I could listen to her lungs. I heard severe breath sounds I asked her to lean over the bed so I could do percussion which is to break up and loosed in the mucus in the lungs.

Janice and I anointed her with oil and prayed for her right there in her bedroom. Janice said she felt a release of the Spirit and I saw in the Spirit realm waves washing up and down the lining of her lungs. She still sounded bad but we were in agreement that her lungs were healed. I told Faye I would try talk to a pulmonologist on Monday and have me seen quickly. The pulmonologist said the quickest way to be seen would be to go to the Emergency Department at St. Francis Bartlett. I called Faye and she left for the ED.

When I arrived at the ED, Faye had been taken for a chest x-ray and they had done blood work. I went to the desk and as the Lord would have it, the doctor when I asked about Faye's lungs said, "Oh, her lungs are clear!" I said, "Are you sure?" She said, "Would you like to see the film and listen to the report of the radiologist?" I saw and heard the report. The doctor said her lungs are clear, it her sodium that is the problem. A nephrologist was called in for her kidneys. Her admission sodium was 119. The next morning her sodium level was 99. The normal is 135 to 145. The nephrologist said I want to recheck you sodium because you are not talking and acting like a person with sodium that low. It was rechecked. The sodium is regulated closely by the kidneys. She should have had seizures and in a coma, not comprehending. The devil made another mistake. When he tried to take her breath, we prayed for her. Then he went for her kidney, he attacked a value that could not be seen but could be deadly. Satan always makes a mistake.

Faye stayed in the hospital for five days and when she left she had 60% kidney function. (End of Annetta's Account)

When I got home, I began meditating and asked the Holy Spirit what the prophetic word spoken over me meant. The crown (means authority and reward) being place on my head meant to me I was being rewarded with clarity of mind and no damage being done to my mind through this illness with possible seizures and potential coma. The waterfall (means spirit and source) was living water in the spirit and in the natural was the kidneys. The purple ribbon (color purple means royalty and rule) represented an unfurling of heavenly protection over a daughter of the Most High God. It was a placing of things in order before they happened.

I recovered from the sodium episode by the end of August. On September 12th, I had ruptured two discs in my back. I had back surgery on September 16th, was doing well, then on October 21st I had new back pain. I had an appointment on October 23rd for a post-op exam. At 3 a.m. on the 23rd I took a pain pill, by 7 a.m. I had begun to have riggers and fever. The doctor said however, that I did not have a ruptured disc but if the pain didn't go away by October 29th, he would do another MRI. After returning home at 12 noon, I took another ½ pain pill, went to sleep, and then I took another ½ pain pill at 4 p.m. I went to sleep *again* and Bob could not arouse me. He became concerned and asked Phyllis and Randy to come up. The next thing I know, they called the ambulance and took me to the emergency room. I was alert by that time. The hospital sent me home and did not take a urine specimen. I continued to have high fever and riggers for the next four days. The family was so concerned about me that Darlene called my PC and told them I was too sick to sit in the waiting room. They said to bring me and they would have someone meet me with a wheelchair and put me in a bed (the favor of the Lord). They tried to put an IV in my arm but after several tries decided they could not. I was sent to the hospital with a "rip roaring urinary tract infection". We were told to not even stop at home to go straight to the hospital. Another favor of the Lord was that I was immediately seen when I arrived at the emergency room. After more tests, they put me in the Intensive Care Step-Down Unit. Of course, Annetta was there before she went to work to visit with me and happened to know by the attending nurse which granted me more favor. I was on antibiotics for nine days fighting the infection. My diagnosis was Acute Urinary Tract Infection with Sepsis. There were two people that died with this after I came home from the hospital. God truly had His hands on me. He is not finished with me yet. My back has continued to hurt so the doctor ordered a Gallian scan to see if there was any infection in my body and where it was located. The test came back with no infection in my back but around my kidneys.

My back continued to hurt and I slept in my chair for many weeks. Lou and Annetta attended a Bill Johnson conference in Franklin, TN on December 6th. While they were there, healing for back pain was called out. Instructions were given to the congregation to call anyone they knew who was suffering with back pain. Lou called me and I was prayed for during this ministry time. I was told to do something that I had not been able to do. I had not been able to lie on my bed on my back. This was what I attempted to do and was not able to lie there for very long. On Sunday, December 7th, Pastor Temke prayed for me and it seemed that the pain increased. On December 9th however, I was able to sleep in my bed for the first time in months. The prayer of faith truly does heal the sick as we are told

in the book of James. *Thank you for your prayers. God is not moved by great need but Great Faith.*

I have been tested and truly have walked through the shadow of death over

the last six months. As I look back over the days, the Word of God has become

active, alive, and working in my life. Even though I was so sick, my spirit was

refreshed and nurtured by the sweetness of the Lord. Jesus is the same yesterday,

today, and forever. He is still healing bodies in 2009.

A Look Ahead (2010 and beyond):
A Continued Focus on Healing, Missions, Music, and Prayer.

Members of River of Life Assembly of God Church continue to offer "A Place of Healing" through service to the local community and support to missions around the world. Examples of local community service include a food bank where more than 400 Tipton County residents receive food every month. The food bank, originally started in 2001, is currently led by Director Jean Geary and Assistant Director Judy Brooks.

River of Life has an extensive missions outreach into more than 60 areas around the world. Because of this global reach, the sun never sets on the mission's ministry of River of Life Church. Support for missionaries around the world include Belgium, Cambodia, China, Colombia, Costa Rica, Ecuador, Guatemala, Kenya, Iceland, India, Indonesia, Ireland, Jamaica, Jordan, Philippines, Scotland, Tanzania, Uruguay, and Venezuela.

Many of those interviewed for this book spoke about the importance of missions. Lifetime member and current Munford Mayor, Dwayne Cole, said that River of Life has always been a strong mission's church. "It's very significant to me that in the Assemblies of God, every program for every age level includes a ministry of missions" (D. Cole, personal interview, October 3, 2013).

Since March 2003, River of Life has been directly involved with a missionary project in Belize, following the work originally started by missionaries Dean and Paulette Jones in 1989. The first convert, Amilcar Dela Rosa, is the leader of the ministry in Buena Vista, Belize; and his brother, Leonel Dela Rosa, pastors the second church in Bella Vista. Both churches are flourishing under their guidance with more than 200 in regular attendance.

Although the national language is English, the ministry is primarily for Spanish speakers. Since 2003, River of Life Church members have made more than 25 mission trips to Belize. A third church is under construction in Unitedville with a completion date expected in 2014. Leaders at River of Life Church are excited about what God is doing in Belize and believe many more souls will be brought into the kingdom through this growing missionary outreach. More information about River of Life Church in Belize is available at https://sites.google.com/a/unitedvilleriveroflife.org/unitedvilleriverof lfe-org/

A new ministry started in October 2013 is Iglesia El Faro (Lighthouse Church) led by Jose and Irma Garcia. This ministry will be located in nearby Millington, TN, and we look forward to seeing God use this Spanish-speaking ministry to carry out His will in our local communities. More information about El Faro Iglesia is available at http://elfarotn.webs.com/

Another new ministry, designed to help the deaf and hard of hearing, is closed captioning for Sunday morning services. "Text on Top is a wireless, affordable software and hardware solution that provides real-time captioning on top of any application running on the secondary computer and without interfering with the use of this secondary computer" (Text on Top, 2013). This cutting-edge technology is so new that River of Life was only the 22nd church in the U.S. to use this software to close caption services. Lucinda Plexico offers this service using the same skills she provides at the University of Memphis and other areas throughout the region. Closed captioning, in addition to sign language, allows Lucinda the opportunity to use her passion serving the deaf and hard of hearing community.

Every member of the church is encouraged to serve in at least one ministry, and there is an opportunity for everyone including children, drama, greeter, media, men, military support, motorcycle, music, nursery, youth, prayer team, Sunday School, usher, women, and just about any other opportunity one can imagine. If there is an interest in serving the community, church leaders are open to creating a new ministry if that is what it takes to help people carry out God's will for their life.

Pastor Dale "Baldeagle" Berryman and his wife, Susan, answered the call to reach the motorcycle community through a local ministry called "APW (All Patches Welcome) Biker Church." Members meet every Sunday afternoon and offer an open house the second Friday of every month. They also reach the biking community by going to bike rallies and organizing fellowship rides. The ministry shares the love of Jesus with everyone, and many of their members are active in River of Life Church.

Church members are also encouraged to get connected through small groups which are offered around the local area throughout the week. John and Jo Anna Wells lead 12 teams of deacons who help people become part of the local body and minister to them as needed. Small groups and the deacon ministry are expected to gain increased importance as the church continues to grow.

Prayer continues to be a large part of what church members are known for according to John Wells. "This church has been called on when there is a prayer need. That has been the case for years, and it still is. I really believe this is a place of prayer" (J. Wells, personal interview, May 30, 2013).

As "A Place of Healing," River of Life members understand that healing is more than physical. It is also spiritual and emotional. Building on more than 85 years of service, River of Life will continue to seek out God's will meeting the needs of the local community and missions around the world healing the soul, spirit, mind, and body.

Sources: http://www.munfordriveroflife.com/ and www.facebook.com/munfordriveroflife

Historical events from the 2010s (source: U.S. Census Bureau)

- President of the United States: Barack Obama
- Population: 308,745,538
- On January 12, 2010, a 7.0 magnitude earthquake devastates Haiti, killing more than 100,000.
- On January 27, 2010, Apple Computer unveils the iPad tablet.
- In February 2010, a series of winter storms labeled "Snowmageddon" blankets the east coast of the United States with up to 40 inches of snow in less than 1 week.
- On August 31, 2010, President Obama formally declares an end to combat operations in Iraq.
- *Time Magazine* announces Facebook founder Mark Zuckerberg as its 2010 Person of the Year.
- U.S. Representative Gabrielle Giffords and 17 others are shot by a gunman during a "Congress on Your Corner" event held on January 8, 2011, in Tucson, AZ.
- A 9.0 magnitude earthquake strikes Japan on March 11, 2011. The quake and subsequent tsunami devastate the Oshika Peninsula of Tohoku.
- On May 2, 2011, U.S. Navy Seals raid a residence in Abbottabad, Pakistan, killing the United State's most wanted terrorist—Osama Bin Laden.
- The launch of Space Shuttle Endeavour (STS-134) on May 16, 2011, marks its last mission to space and the second to last shuttle mission before the end of the space shuttle program.

Cost of living (Source: The People History)

New Home	$232,880
Gasoline	$2.73
Bacon (1 pound)	$2.97
Eggs (1 dozen)	$1.37
Loaf of Bread	$2.49

Food bank volunteers serve more than 400 Tipton County residents every month.

Honorbound Men's Ministry fellowship opportunities include skeet shooting and other activities that encourage mentoring youth.

Pastor Jacob Winegardner   Rich Bierwirth

Every fellowship opportunity includes a lesson from God's Word, including this one from Munford Mayor Dwayne Cole.

Honorbound Men's Ministry Skeet Shoot

Johnny Combs

Gaylon Combs

Jeremy Payant

Mayor Dwayne Cole

Pastor Greg Temke

Honorbound Men's Ministry 2011 Skeet Shoot
Youth and Adult Champions.

Luigi Favazza, Michael Ellison, and Jordan Combs

Jeremy Payant, Alvin Plexico, and Erik Caldwell

Honorbound Men's Ministry offers prayer every year at Munford
Celebrate. This outreach is one way church members serve the
local community.

Mayor Dwayne Cole and David Wolle

Bob Greathouse

James Armstrong

Honorbound Men's Ministry offers a father-son fishing event as part of their sponsorship of Royal Rangers.

Jeremy Payant

Rich Bierwirth

Tyler and Stan High

Authentic Youth Ministry
led by Pastor Jacob and Sarah Winegardner
is focused on connecting young people who want to know the real
meaning of life and the answer to real problems teenagers have.

Authentic Youth is a wonderful opportunity for youth to get together and be real with each other. No phoniness here! It is a chance for kids to have fun, make friendships, find encouragement, and dig down to connect with the real meaning of life.

APW (All Patches Welcome) Biker Church led by
Pastor Dale "Baldeagle" and Susan Berryman

The Leader Church of the Week

w.covingtonleader.com

Th

of Life Church is located at at 220 Beaver Road in Munford. Worship – 10 a.m., Sunday School ..m., Wednesday night 7 p.m. The church also has Kingdom Warriors Children's Ministry and X- ..e youth. A nursery is provided for all services and transportation is available by calling 840- ... For more information visit the website at www.munfordriveroflifechurch.com

Belize River of Life Pastor Amilcar and Family

Belize River of Life Kingdom Expansion Conference

River of Life leaders in 2013 included Senior Pastors, Greg and Bonnie Temke; Children's Pastors, Greg and Paula DeVaughn; and Youth Pastors, Jacob and Sarah Winegardner.

PASTOR'S LETTER 2013

Dear Church Family,

It is my pleasure to share with you the blessings that have occurred at River of Life during the 2012 - 2013 year. I can say with great certainty, God has blessed us beyond measure. *James 1:17 says, "Every good gift and every perfect gift is from above; it comes down from the Father above."* God has given many gifts to River of Life and they are the people who attend. The gifts of God come in the form of people who worship and fellowship at River of Life Church.

Each church has a different calling as to the purposes of God for that local congregation. River of Life is a church of healing for the spirit, soul, and body. We believe that God sends in people who are broken, bruised, and battered and the Lord makes them whole!

SPIRITUAL

We have record of 19 adults, 38 children, and 16 teens who have made professions of faith and now attend River of Life on a regular basis. There were additional salvations recorded in our services and other outreach ministries, but this number represents those attending ROL currently. Several of our new converts were baptized in the Holy Spirit, with the evidence of speaking in other tongues.

We also had the privilege of seeing 11 people baptized in water. We have received 22 new members into our fellowship at River of Life which brings our membership total to 156. There were 7 baby dedications, 5 weddings, and sadly 6 funerals. Church attendance average stands at 245 for 2013, which represents a 10% increase over year previous. 142 recorded visitors have attended our services thus far in 2013.

We recognize that all blessings have come from regular times of prayer and fasting. These special times of prayer, fasting, and intercession are the fundamental way that God's hand of blessing is seen on our church body.

GIVING

Please look over the financial reports to see the Lord's blessings in the area of tithes and offerings this past year. Our general fund giving was recorded at *$407,045.00*, which was a *3.5%* increase over the previous year. Budgets were exceeded by gross revenues of *$12,302.00*. Total receipts for 2012-2013 were recorded at *$642,251.00*. Our outstanding debt was increased in November of 2012 by *$51,000* and has since been reduced to *$76,402.00* at the time of this report.

Significant strides were made on our physical plant with nearly *$155,160.00* spent on *building maintenance, building upgrades, building equipment, and special projects.* Total gross building expenses stood at *$217,827.00* or *33%* of total expenses.

This past year has seen increased commitment with River of Life's missions vision. We held a total of 10 missions services and 5 new missionaries were added to our regular *Monthly Missionary Support List.* Missions giving saw a *$2,472.00 decrease* over the year previous, a *-2.5% decrease.* Belize Missions registered a *$4,974.00 decrease* in giving or a *-5% drop.* We have seen a significant increase of outside giving to Belize through our relationship with Partnership International. This relationship has enabled the Belize church to be completed with the dedicatory service planned for

February 2014. The Food Bank client list has grown to over 1,100 with an average of 400+ families receiving monthly assistance. Total missions giving to World Missions and Belize stood at **$187,141.00** representing **29%** of total receipts, an incredible number! To God be the glory!

January 2014 will be a time to once again revisit and refocus our commitment to World Missions, when Rev. Bruce Headley visits ROL.

ADDITIONAL MINISTRIES AND OUTREACHES
Fall Festival/Trunk or Treat Outreach, 1,000 +
Veteran's Day Dinner Celebration, 160 in attendance
Revival with JR Gould, 8 baptized in the Holy Spirit
Vacation Bible School, over 25 children visited for first time and many received Christ

We are excited about the biker church that Dale and Susan Berryman have established on Quintin Drive, in Munford. The A.P.W. Biker Church stands for *"All Patches Welcome" Biker Church*. We are excited about the Widow's Mite ministry headed by Sheila Templeman. We are excited about the prayer cloths that Frances Gannon is sending to our U.S. troops. We are excited about the prayer cloths being sent to hospitals by Gail Honagel. We are excited about many things!

PERSONAL REPORT

Preached 82 x's at ROL	13 Elder Council meetings
4 Deacon Meetings	4 Leadership Meetings
1 Deacon Training	15 Staff Meetings
10 Food Bank Distribution Days	7 Youth Leadership Trainings
1 All Church Business Meeting	6 Funerals
3 Weddings	4 Sectional Minister's Meetings
2 Munford Minister's Meetings	2 Training Weeks with Wayne and Sharon Lee
Preached in Covington Section 2x's	Attended 4 Special District Committee Meetings
Taught Corinthians Ordination Class	

The year was filled with many joys and victories! Seeing souls walk to the altar is the greatest gift that I could ever ask for as a pastor. The church staff and department leaders continue to bless me as we minister together. I thank them for their commitment to the Lord Jesus and ROL Church. It is a personal privilege of mine to labor together on a weekly basis with the people we have here. A significant team is being woven together that will bring kingdom impact for many years to come.

I want to thank each of you for calling River of Life your home church. This is truly a *Place of Family*, and it continues to be a *Place of Healing*. It is a privilege to serve you. I view it as a sacred trust and try never to take it lightly. River of Life is a very healthy church and for that we give God the glory. It is a fun place to attend church, make friends, and love Jesus. I believe every person in Munford, Atoka, Drummonds, and Brighton should attend! God has helped River of Life not only heal, but God has helped River of Life grow in ministries and maturity.

To God be the glory,

Pastor Greg Temke

BELIZE REPORT
August 2012 to July 2013

We have had a great year of ministry in Belize. Since August 2012, Partnership International has sent a total of eight teams there. They have done everything from feeding programs to building updates.

Our new building, in Unitedville, has progressed from a slab and shell to a complete building with walls, doors, and a roof. Also, a front entrance has been completed. There is temporary electrical service to the building being run from one of the cabanas. We are hopeful to have the kitchen, windows, and electrical service completed by February 2014 for the dedication of the building.

Pastor Greg and I spent a week there ministering in April 2013. It was a time used for preaching in our churches and gathering information to further the work.

Amilcar Dela Rosa has done an excellent job overseeing the Belize churches. We moved the church in Buena Vista to the new property located in Unitedville.

1. Buena Vista to Unitedville: 200 people in attendance, 20 saved, 15 filled with the Holy Spirit, 32 baptized in water
2. Bella Vista: 90 people in attendance, 45 saved, 40 filled with the Holy Spirit, 28 baptized in water. Some of these were saved in revivals and attend other churches. Walls are up on the expansion, now ready for the roof.
3. Mango Creek: New work, 20 people in attendance
4. Mayamopan: 6 month old Myan church, 75 people in attendance
5. Armenia: Mayan church 1 1/2 years old, 80 people in attendance, side walls now complete on 30' x 50' structure
6. San Roman: New work, first service scheduled for October 13th, 60 people ready to attend this Myan/English church

Thank you for your continued support of the Belize ministry. Please be praying for our upcoming trip in February.

Respectfully submitted,

Bill Greathouse

Deacon Ministry
2012 - 2013

Twelve groups (teams) comprised of twenty-five people are serving as a deacon/deaconess. The purpose of this ministry is to let the people who attend ROL on a regular basis know that someone misses and prays for them. More people are needed to help us in this ministry, especially in the area of our shut-ins and nursing home residents. It is not a huge time consuming job, but does require some follow-up calls, emails, or visits as needed. Most of our members require very little from us since they are already so faithful and devoted to our Lord.

Serving are: (1) Dale & Susan Berryman & Deborah Dawson; (2) Gaylon & Carolyn Combs; (3) Shirley Conlee & Rheba McDaniel; (4) Allen & Barbara Hanks; (5) J.T. & Bonnie Forbess; (6) Stan & Teresa High; (7) Peggy Cox, Dotty Rice & Martha Watkins; (8) Lou Grasser & Mary Alice Starnes; (9) Ed & Clara Mynatt; (10) Linda Patrick & Beatrice Wyatt; (11) Deborah Kirchoff; (12) Darren & Christine Wallace. A HUGE thanks to all of them for "walking in the good works" which God has ordained for each of us to do.

John Earl & Jo Anna Wells

ANNUAL SUNDAY SCHOOL REPORT
August 1, 2012 to July 31, 2013

I wish to thank everyone connected with Sunday School. That is teachers, helpers, and attendees as it takes us all to make a successful Sunday School.

We have made progress this year. We have several new classes and new teachers. Attendance has averaged 118 per Sunday with a total enrollment of 194.

Respectfully,

Martha Watkins

Youth Pastor's Report

This last year has been a year of growth, not only numerically but spiritually. I have to admit I am much more concerned with spiritual growth than numerical, because the spiritual growth makes much more of an impact. Many things went on this year so it's hard to single out one specific thing to mention. I will just tell you how our services have been for the last year.

Our biggest push in the youth ministry of River of Life Church has been worship. We have been pushing our students to press into the presence of God and catch a glimpse of the limitless possibilities He can produce, to feel the revival fire that so deeply burns within the heart of God and the leadership of the youth, and to lead others into this worship, too! This next year, the adult and students leaders will play an even greater roll in the ministry of Authentic Youth. It is my heart and desire to not only discover future ministers within the youth group but to also give them opportunities to minister. Every month, at least once a month, an adult or student leader will bring the Word to our students. This is a vital part of our vision to grow the youth through the leadership of Authentic Youth. Discipleship time and Bible study has grown our students to a greater level, a level which we have never before seen. To all of this, I thank God. He has proven Himself faithful!

In this next year, our plan and vision is to equip leaders to build and lead leaders, to create a culture of worship, devotion to God, prayer, and reading the Word. Building the youth group through the core belief that devotion to God encompasses our entire life and who we are, not just on Wednesdays and Sundays, but every moment of our lives. We are going to portray that God and the Holy Spirit are available all the time, in every moment of our life, and in every situation. Because of this vision, we are currently developing students that are hungry for more of God. Training them in the Word and prayer, we are continuing to go after those who are waining and always keeping an eye out for the new ones. We are also believing God for 100 hungry, excited, and motivated youth in this coming year. We know God can do it and we are believing He will! This next year looks promising, not because of the leadership of Authentic Youth, but because God is and will always be faithful to the very end. Amen!

So expect to see more and more students flooding into Authentic Youth and if you don't know their names remember just to say "What up!" Thank you for letting Mrs. Sarah and I be your youth pastors!

Pastor Jacob Winegardner

IMAGINE KIDS MINISTRY 2013

This year has been a year of transition for our ministry. Many of the children we began with, have grown and flew out of our nest in Youth and Sunday morning services. Ours is a ministry of planting seeds for others to harvest. However, we have a new crop of little ones entering our Sunday morning and Wednesday night services. We have been blessed to have Debbie Rowland, Stacie McMullen, Amanda Holloway, Patricia Murphy, Megan Berryman and Jennifer Kelly step into the leadership role of Imagine Kids Jr, our preschool program.

The summer of 2013 brought two new adventures for us. For Kids Camp we took 15 kids to the Tennessee district Camp Jackson. It was like going home. We had six first time salvations or rededications. We had three become baptized by the Holy Spirit. The next week back home at ROL, we held an Adult/Kid VBS. We had an average attendance of sixty. Thank you Tiffany Carroll for an outstanding job as VBS director.

We are looking forward to all God has for Imagine Kids in 2014. We stand in faith that God can use us in ways we cannot think or imagine.

In Christ,

Greg and Paula DuVaughn

ANNUAL RIVER OF LIFE WOMEN'S MINISTRIES REPORT

August 1, 2013 to July 31, 2013

It's been another amazing year for Women's Ministries at River of Life Church. Our mission is to reach, disciple, fellowship, and mentor women of all ages, diverse backgrounds, and ethnic groups. Historically, women at River of Life assist others whether it's by a touch, a prayer, a call, a visit, or leading or attending a small group.

We have corporate meetings for our women usually eight times a year where we fellowship and have a devotional by one of our anointed ladies. This year the focus has been to incorporate the younger women, as they have so much to give and the older women can learn and share. Our theme from the National Assemblies of God Women's Ministries is "Redeemed: Transformation". We are celebrating our uniqueness in our meetings. God created each and every one of us with unique talents, gifts, and special ways to minister to women. Our speakers are giving their own individual perspective on how the Lord has worked in them and how we can minister to others using our own unique talents.

We, at River of Life, have been a busy group of women this year. Our planning committee met several times during the year to plan events or projects to assist in growing the kingdom of God through WMs. We had our first leadership planning retreat in August at the Greathouse Bed & Breakfast where we prayerfully sought God's plan for WMs for the coming year. We all had a wonderful time of fun and fellowship. We also take the stewardship of our funds very seriously and prayerfully.

The following are a few projects/purchases WMs have made:

- We had our annual retreat at ROL, with our children's pastor's wife, Paula Devaughn as the keynote speaker. We had a wonderful time of praise and worship.
- We celebrated our fourth annual Ruby Dinner in February and had a special night of fellowship together with our Honor Bound Men serving us in an extravagant way!
- We donated and bought Christmas bags and baskets or goodies/personal items for the Women's Recovery Center at Rose of Sharon.
- We decorated the infant nursery with furniture and décor ($500.00)
- We sent three children to children's camp.
- We sent two youth to youth camp.
- We sent two women to the state WMs conference.
- We purchased five round tables for the fellowship hall for dinners and fellowship.

The list of all the ways our women minister is too numerous to report. A small sampling is:

- Funeral dinner preparation and serving
- Baby/Wedding showers given
- A craft class being taught and shared
- A small group where women share Bible studies
- Meals prepared and delivered for the sick or homebound
- A call when someone is grieving or hurting through a loss
- Praying for healing
- Filling bags and praying for our Food Bank recipients
- Taking the time to attend Women Ministry meetings
- Giving to the poor whether time or money
- Ministering to a diverse group
- Motorcycle ministry
- Praise & Worship leaders and members
- Widows Mite meals and dinners for our widows

As director of the Women's Ministries of River of Life, I stand in awe of what giving, loving, and prayerful women we have working for the Lord's Kingdom. I am so thankful to be a small part of the whole. We are truly here to serve in whatever capacity needed and we invite all women to come be a part of Women's Ministry!

Respectfully,

Annetta Parker

HONORBOUND MEN'S REPORT
August 1, 2012 to July 31, 2013

The past twelve months have been filled with many activities and events focused on men. HonorBound Men's Ministries is dedicated to the development and forging of men for service to Christ. Each activity and event is designed to challenge men to grow in their relationship with God, their families, and other men.

Highlights of the past year include:

Hosted the Covington Section LFTL Banquet
Supported the Royal Ranger program at ROL Church
Hosted men's breakfast events
Hosted HBMM booth at Celebrate Munford
Hosted Veterans' Day celebration with luncheon
Assisted men in financial crisis

Our stated goals for the next twelve months are:

Focus all activities on one purpose—Win Men (Specific goal 10 men)
Increase event/activity participation to average 65 men
Develop small groups for men
Broaden the men's leadership team to include others

As we move forward, it is our desire that each man at ROL Church connect with other men in HBMM. By recognizing the value of male friends, men are better able to face the challenges of the day-to-day warfare we all encounter. We cannot afford to have men only attend our services without connecting with other men in a small group setting. Our goal is to develop HBMM into a relationship based ministry.

Respectfully,

Co-Directors
Dwayne Cole
Bill Greathouse

ELDERS & WIVES:
Bill & Jan Greathouse
David & Marilyn Wolle
Jack & Tiffany Carroll
Lou & Annetta Parker
Tim & Aless Trumbo
Bob & Faye Ellis, Elder Emeritus

SUNDAY SCHOOL STAFF:
Tiffany Carroll, Superintendent
Jean Geary, Nursery
Deborah Dawson, 3 & 4 yr. old
Teresa Tutor, 5 yr. old
Melody Bierwirth, 1st & 2nd Grades
Becky Colvett, 3rd & 4th Grades
Sandy Coley, 5th & 6th Grade
Tracie Minear, 6th-8th Grade
Jacob & Sarah Winegardner, 9-12th Grade
David & Mary Espinoza, Young Adults & Couples
Sheila Templeman, Overcomers' Class
Linda Patrick, Adult Elective
J. T. Forbess, Adult Teacher
Jennifer Poston, Assistant Teacher
Joan Billings, Assistant Teacher
Deborah Kirchoff, Assistant Teacher
Bill Oswalt, Assistant Teacher
Dwayne Cole, Men's Adult Elective
Janice Greathouse, Ladies' Adult Elective
Annetta Parker, Rosemary McCane, Debbie Rowland
Assistant Teachers
Pastor Greg, Victorious Living Class

AUTHENTIC YOUTH MINISTRY:
Jacob & Sarah Winegardner, Pastors
Chandler Kirchoff, Helper
Lindsey Combs, Helper
Megan Berryman, Helper
Melanie Glass, Helper
David Wolle, Helper

IMAGINE KIDS' MINISTRY:
Greg & Paula DeVaughn, Pastors
Megan Berryman, Helper
Jacob Coley, Helper
Jonah DeVaughn, Helper
Mac & Lisa Kail, Helpers
Stan, Teresa, Tyler High, Helpers
Jennifer Kelly, Teacher
Elizabeth Painter, Teacher
Debbie Rowland, Teacher
Tracie Minear, Teacher
Hannah & Leah Minear, Teacher

WOMEN'S MINISTRY:
Annetta Parker, Director

HONOR BOUND MEM'S MINISTRY:
Dwayne Cole, Bill Greathouse, Directors

USHERS & GREETERS:
Ralph Templeman, Head Usher
Mike Murphy, Head Greeter
Al & Rose Lightfoot, Greeters
Alvin Plexico, Usher
Bill Oswalt, Usher
Bob & Faye Ellis, Greeters
Chandler Kirchoff, Greeter
Chris & Valerie Guy, Greeters
Dale & Susan Berryman, Greeters
Daniel Mayer, Greeter
Darren & Christine Wallace, Greeters
Dotty Rice, Greeter
Ed & Clara Mynatt, Greeters
Greg Cox, Greeter
Jack Carroll, Usher
John Erb. Greeter
Jonah DeVaughn, Usher
Lewis & Rosemary McCane, Greeters
Lou & Annetta Parker, Usher/Greeter
Melanie Glass, Greeter
Michael Ellison, Usher
Patricia Murphy, Greeter
Peggy Cox, Greeter
Scott & Margie O'Nan, Greeters

USHERS & GREETERS (Continued):
Sean & Tracie Minear, Greeters
Tim Wheeler, Usher

SOUND BOOTH:
Tim Trumbo, Sound Director
Jeremy Payant, Media Director
Brian Holloway, Technician
Jeff Colvett, Technician
Shawn Walther, Technician

MUSIC & PRAISE TEAM:
Bonnie Temke, Director

Singers:
Aless Trumbo
Jennifer Poston
Betsy Kelsey
Elizabeth Painter
Jacob Winegardner

Piano/Keyboard:
Sarah Winegardner
Andrew Wolle

Drums:
Jacob Winegardner
Jonah DeVaughn
Terry Dawson

Guitar:
Kevin Giles
Nick Jordan
David Wolle

DRAMA MINISTRY:
Terry Dawson, Director

FOOD BANK MINISTRY:
Jean Geary, Director
Judy Brooks, Assistant Director
John Wells, Assistant
Peggy Cox, Assistant

COMMUNION PREP:
Charles Hambick

HOSPITALITY;
Darren & Christine Wallace

KITCHEN COORDINATOR:
Rose Lightfoot

MIGHTY & WISE DIRECTORS:
Rev. Bill & Lou Oswalt

ROYAL RANGER/MPACT MINISTRIES:
Greg & Paula DeVaughn, Directors
Rich Bierwirth, RR Coordinator
Lisa Kail, M'Pact Coordinator
Janice Greathouse, Helper
Jennifer Kelley, Teacher
Crystal Seeber, Helper
Lelah Harmon, Teacher
Valerie Guy, Teacher
Jeremy Payant, Teacher
Mac Kail, Teachers
Melody Bierwirth, Teacher

NURSERY:
Jean Geary, Director

DEACON/DEACONESS MINISTRY:
John & Jo Anna Wells, Directors
Raven Belue
Dale & Susan Berryman
Gaylon & Carolyn Combs
Shirley Conlee
Peggy Cox
David & Mary Espinoza
Deborah Dawson
J.T. & Bonnie Forbess
Bill & Jan Greathouse
Lou Grasser
Allen & Barbara Hanks
Stan & Teresa High
Deborah Kirchoff

DEACON/DEACONESS MINISTRY (continued):
Rheba McDaniel
Ed & Clara Mynatt
Linda Patrick
Dotty Rice
Mary Alice Starnes
Darren & Christine Wallace
Martha Watkins
Beatrice Wyatt

FINANCIAL COMMITTEE:
Carolyn Combs
Peggy Cox
Bill Greathouse
Deborah Kirchoff
Jennifer Poston

PAID STAFF

Full Time:
Rev. Greg Temke, Senior Pastor
Bill Greathouse, Administrator
Rev. Jacob & Sarah Winegardner, Youth Pastors

Part Time:
Greg & Paula DeVaughn, Children's Pastors
Jennifer Poston, Treasurer
Janice Greathouse, Secretary
Judy Brooks, Janitorial
Jean Geary, Janitorial, Nursery
Mary Alice Starnes, Office Assistant

Pastors of Munford River of Life First Assembly of God Church

Raymond F. Wiseman	February 3, 1929 – March 27, 1930
William Bridges	March 27, 1930
Brother Anderson	1930s
Brother Foshee	1930s
Brother Firkins	1930s
Brother Findley	1930s
Brother Berryhill	1930s
R. L. Wilkerson	1930s
Brother Salyers	1930s
Eluis King	1930s
W. E. Lindsey	1930s
Claude McKeel	1930s
T. J. Lemons	1930s
Paul McKeel	1943-1947
George Preslar	1947-1951
J. W. Gladney	1951-1953
Earl Pritchard	February 1953 – March 1963
E. R. Driver	March 1963 – June 1966
C. M. Hicks	August 1966 – October 1972
Wayne Bradley	1972 – 1975
Charles Hurst	June 1975 – August 1984
J. David Stone	October 1985 – March 1987
Windell Splawn	March 1987 – July 1991
Gene Burgess	August 1991 – 1999
James Laymon	May 2000 – October 2007
Greg Temke	August 2008 - Present